Also by Leslie Hamilton

365 Four-Star Videos You (Probably) Haven't Seen

The Cheapskate's Guide to Living Cheaper and Better

Leslie Hamilton

A Citadel Press Book
Published by Carol Publishing Group

A Citadel Press Book
Published by Carol Publishing Group
Citadel Press is a registered trademark of Carol Communications, Inc.

Editorial, sales and distribution, rights and permissions inquiries should be addressed to Carol Publishing Group, 120 Enterprise Avenue, Secaucus, N.J. 07094. In Canada: Canadian Manda Group, One Atlantic Avenue, Suite 105, Toronto, Ontario M6K 3E7

Carol Publishing Group books are available at special discounts for bulk purchases, sales promotion, fund-raising, or educational purposes. Special editions can be created to specifications. For details, contact: Special Sales Department, Carol Publishing Group, 120 Enterprise Avenue, Secaucus, N.J. 07094

Manufactured in the United States of America

10 9 8 7 6 5 4 3 2 1

Library of Congress Cataloging-in-Publication Data

Hamilton, Leslie. 1950–
    The cheapskate's guide to living cheaper and better / Leslie Hamilton.
        p. cm.
    "A Citadel Press book."
    ISBN 0–8065–1795–6 (pbk.)
    1. Consumer education. 2. Home economics—Accounting. I. Title
TX335.H3433 1996
640'.42—dc20   95–48054
                                                            CIP

When poverty comes (as it sometimes will) upon the prudent, the industrious, and the well-informed, a judicious education is all-powerful in enabling them to endure the evils it cannot always prevent. A mind full of piety and knowledge is always rich; it is a bank that never fails; it yields a perpetual dividend of happiness.

—From *The Frugal Housewife (Dedicated to Those Who Are Not Ashamed of Economy)* by "Mrs. Child," 1833

Contents

Acknowledgments

My grateful thanks go to my husband Bob, to Hank and Mary Tragert, to Brandon Toropov, and to the rest of the clan for all their help and advice: Anne Tragert, Mary Tragert Toropov, John Tragert, Kathy Tragert, Matthew Tragert, Elizabeth Tragert, Chris Tragert, Suzanne Tragert, Joseph Tragert and Bernadine Tragert; (and it's about time, too!) to Mike and Kathryn Geoffrion-Scannell, Margaret Geoffrion, Tracee Kneeland-Swanson, Donna McAffee-Bassett, Tasia Knudsen, Pete Knudsen, Shawna Behnke, Wensley Hefni, Mark Waldstein (he who knows whereof he speaks) and Tami Forman. I'd also like to thank my mother, Leslie Hamilton, Fran McHugh, and my dad, "Red" Hamilton, and my grandmother Katherine Stout.

Introduction

Is it your imagination, or does the world at large seem to conspire to keep you from putting even a little money away? Does it seem as though your friends always have cash on hand *and* the newest in high-tech stereo equipment, *and* a TV the size of a drive-in theater? Their cars run as smoothly as their apparently perfect lives. What gives? And why do you feel the unmistakeable urge to throttle your friends from time to time?

Before things get serious, take action. Soon, after following some of the simple steps outlined in this book, you, too, will be able to hold your head high, splurge occasionally on the latest high-tech toys, and make others green with envy. And you won't go bankrupt in the process, either. Because you'll be focusing on the best values, not just the best stuff. Sounds like fun, doesn't it? Well, it is. Because the only thing better than having something really cool is *getting it for next to nothing*.

Spending less and *improving* your standard of living is possible. The ideas in this book prove it! Enjoy them in good health, and try not to flaunt your flourishing condition in front of your friends too much. They could resent it.

The Cheapskate's Guide to
Living Cheaper and Better

1

Balance Your Budget

Managing your money and prioritizing purchases—a topic that makes most of us start shivering and hallucinating about people in visors with large calculating machines. But you can relax; everything that follows is painless.

We'll start the book with a few smart choices in managing your money, steps you can take right now—as well as a few pieces of simple, pragmatic advice on how to save money in your daily routine. In this part of the book, you'll learn to simplify your financial situation and plan your budget for almost any eventuality. By following the advice in this section, you'll be well on the way to being able to afford what you need—and having a little money in the bank to boot.

- Learn the difference between *needing* something and *wanting* something. Blurring these distinctions turns practical decisions into emotional ones. If you can't afford a particular treat, you weren't meant to have it. Now. If you were meant to have it, it will still be there when you *can* afford it. Make a written list of the things you want to have—eventually. Turn them into rewards you will faithfully bestow on yourself after achieving some mean-ingful, lifestyle-improving goal. Anticipating that cherry red Ferrari can be a powerful motivator, one you can put to work to your benefit! Post a picture of that dazzling automobile on the refrigerator to remind yourself of exactly what you're working toward.

■ If all else fails, take the chicken test. Let's say you desperately need something—a table, for instance. There's no debate. You need this. You've been eating standing up for months, which is fine, but you have company coming for dinner next week, and you have only so much counter space. So you need a table. Okay. You find one at a yard sale for $15. It may not be pretty—now—but with paint and some tightening of joints, you can turn it into something quite nice. There's a problem, though. As you go to pay for the table, you pass a ceramic chicken that's all but clucking out loud for to you to take it home. The chicken costs $35. You don't need the chicken. Your family won't be impressed by the chicken. In terms of improving your standard of living, the chicken isn't as important as some other things you could attend to. You've got to learn to put the chicken back. Constantly ask yourself questions like this: "Do I *need* the chicken or do I *want* the chicken?" Ask questions like this mentally before *every* purchase, especially unplanned ones. Be honest. If necessary, use the chicken as a reward for some later standard-of-living-boosting achievement, one that has at least $35 attached to it. But put it back. For now.

■ Set a goal of saving 10 percent of your pretax income.

■ Try to use your credit card only for big-ticket items; try to pay the balance off the next month if humanly possible.

■ Keep your credit cards in a safe place at home, rather than in your purse or wallet. Preferably, you should place the cards in a container with a very complicated lock, the better to inhibit impulse spending.

■ If you're looking for an "investment" but have not yet paid off your credit card debts, take the money you've saved and pay down your card! Paying down $1,000 on a card with an 18 percent interest rate, you'll save $180 in interest you would otherwise have had to pay. That's a risk-free "return" that's pretty tough to beat.

■ According to *Woman's Day* magazine, paying just $10 more than the minimum payment on a $5,000 credit card debt (at 18 percent interest) yields a financial savings of $4,557 and reduces the monthly payment schedule by more than 18 years.

■ Rank order your debts. Pay off the loans with the highest interest rate (probably that credit card) as quickly as you can, and make the minimum payment to the rest. After that debt is paid, attack the next one just as vigorously.

■ Don't sign up for a low-interest credit card before you learn how long that interest rate last. (A good many cards make you pay the normal, outlandish rates after sixty or ninety days if you don't pay off your balance in full.)

■ You can take advantage of low-interest credit cards without getting hooked. There are dozens of these to choose from. Transfer your balance to one with a low introductory rate, then keep an eye on the expiration date and switch to another low-rate card before it changes. Pay the balance off with the new card. Keep your payments as high as they were when you were paying at the higher interest rate, and you'll be paid off that much quicker. The trick here lies in marking the date that the low "teaser" rate expires—being ready to switch to another card.

- One low-rate card financial experts seem to agree offers very attractive terms is Wachovia Bank's, which, as of this writing, was listed at 9 percent prime for the first year, with the rate escalating to prime plus 3.9 percent after than point. Rates do change, though, so you should probably call them at 800-842-3262 to get all the details.

- Never, never, never use charge cards for small-ticket items like groceries, no matter how convenient it may seem at the time. Write a check or pay cash.

- ATM cards sure are convenient, aren't they? Everywhere you turn, there's a machine that honors yours. Only trouble is, you get charged a nice flat fee for every transaction that doesn't take place on one of your bank's machines, and the fees are often buried in your bank statement in such a way that they look like standard monthly charges. They aren't. Skip the national-network cash machines unless you're facing an emergency. Or find a bank that doesn't charge you these fees.

- Do your income taxes early (i.e., January 2). Uncle Sam isn't paying you any interest on that money that's coming your way—eventually—in the form of a refund.

- Never ignore a letter from the Internal Revenue Service. It's easier to rationalize doing so than you might think. A staggering number of the problem cases at the IRS involve people who simply decided to stop opening the envelopes. Answer the letters, even if your response is a phone call explaining that you don't understand the situation or will be late with a payment.

- Some of the personal-finance software programs out there will allow you to save an hour or so of time, and perhaps twenty stamps a month, by paying your bills directly through your checking account. It adds up—and a good program (like Quicken) will allow you to take command of your personal finances, painlessly and in short order. That's a nice bonus.

- If your company has a 401(k) plan or something like it, take advantage of it. Invest as much money as you comfortably can from each paycheck—before you see the cash. Mark your calendar six months in advance, and consider raising the amount that goes into the account twice a year.

- Meet with a financial adviser to learn whether you'd save on interest payments by refinancing your home.

- Don't send in that tax return yet! There are any number of completely legitimate deductions you may have overlooked. Your hearing aid, for instance, and its batteries, should qualify.

- So should a business-related cellular phone. (And all the calls you make on it!)

- So should expenses you incur by printing and distributing your resumé, as well as any money you spent on an employment agency over the past year to find a job in your established occupation. (No, it doesn't matter whether or not you got a job through the agency.)

- So should educational expenses you incur in order to maintain your skills in your current occupation. (You can't deduct educational expenses meant to help you get ready for a *new* occupation.)

- So should all the money you spent over the past year on contraceptives. (They're a medical expense.)

- So should anything you spent on job-related uniforms. This is an item of particular interest to families with members in the military or in a police or fire department.

■ So should your moving expenses—if you moved in order to start your first job or change jobs, and if you would have otherwise faced a commute that was fifty miles longer.

■ Talk to your tax adviser about any deduction you plan to take, and track down a copy of *The Ernst and Young Tax Guide* (published by John Wiley, 1995), a superior tax guide with all the information you need on deductions people usually overlook.

■ By the way, did you work for more than one employer over the past year? If you did, you should double-check the *total* Social Security taxes withheld before you send in your return. Not claiming the full amount due as a result of overpayment is a common filing error.

■ Yikes! The IRS has called you in for an audit. A word of warning: Some of the people you'll run into downtown will seem *really* nice. Fight the urge to respond to their pleasant, open demeanor with pleasant, exhaustive responses to all the questions. Don't withhold information, but recognize there's money at stake, and that the full implications of the chattiness your conversational partner is trying to encourage may not be obvious to you. Try to answer as many questions as you can with single sentences and words of one or two syllables. Do keep smiling pleasantly, though.

■ Who needs a bank? Check out the cooperatives or savings banks in your area; they may offer the same services your bank offers for a whole lot less. Credit unions also offer great deals. They offer lower fees, lower interest on loans, and easier credit terms. They may also give higher interest rates on investments.

■ Considering a telephone purchase? Never give your credit

card number to a telemarketer unless you called *them*, not vice versa.

■ Estimate how much spending money you'll need each week. Then withdraw that amount of money on Monday and stay away from the bank until next Monday! (Yes, you can revise your estimates from week to week. The idea is to find your amount and stick to it.)

■ Forget about rebates. Who mails them in? Unless you're dealing with a major purchase (like an automobile), consider the list price to be the final price.

■ If you spot a discrepancy in your credit card bill, write the credit card company immediately. Send a separate letter, not just an insertion to your bill. Don't just call. You have specific rights under the Fair Credit Billing Act; if you don't write, you may be held responsible for unauthorized charges.

■ Learn how to deal with manufacturers and get the most for your money. Write for the Consumer's Resource Handbook and the Consumer Assistance Directory. The address: Handbook Publication Request, U.S. Consumer Product Safety Commission, Washington, DC 20207.

■ Read the Consumer's Financial Guide. You can get a free copy by writing the Publications Section, Printing Branch, Stop C-11, Securities and Exchange Commission, 450 Fifth Street NW, Washington, DC 20549.

■ Read the fine print. Then read it again.

■ Want to simplify the decision-making process? Resolve never to buy anything a telemarketer calls you about. Explain that it's "family policy."

■ My favorite way of disconnecting telemarketers before they start talking about something they want me to spend money on? Easy. I just explain that I'd love to hear them out, but I don't have a phone. During the stunned silence, say goodbye and hang up.

■ Round up your mortgage payment to the nearest even number. You'll pay off the principal sooner.

■ Use your library card, rather than your credit card, to keep up with recent bestsellers. And, just to be neighborly, learn the librarian's first name while you're at it. The librarian is one of the most important allies you can make in your neighborhood.

■ Buy a public transit pass; try to use your car only in emergencies or for long trips.

■ For some solid advice on making sense of your family's finances, send a self-addressed, stamped envelope to the Consumer Federation of America at P.O. Box 12099, Washington, DC 20005. You'll get a full list of their helpful publications.

2

Your Home

If you own it, your home has probably cost you anywhere between $30,000 and $200,000+. That's an investment worth taking care of—and adding value to. This doesn't mean putting in an indoor tennis court, or a bathroom worthy of Cleopatra. But there are a few inexpensive projects you can do yourself that will make you money when the time comes to sell, not to mention the reward of a more relaxing and more enjoyable place to live. And many of the ideas that follow can, after appropriate discussions with your landlord, be adapted to apartment life. Remember, you should be reimbursed for your work.

Decorating

Slow down. Nobody, but nobody, moves into a home or apartment and makes it look like a page out of *Architectural Digest* in a week. A home doesn't really begin to take on your character and style for quite a while. Even if you had all the money in the world, a home that slowly evolves into a reflection of your own unique style always comes out better than one that has an all-encompassing predetermined design imposed on it. Don't pressure yourself to get everything done right away. If you're in a hurry, you'll make mistakes, spend more money then you intended to, and end up living in a place that doesn't really reflect who you are.

- Shopping for pots, pans, and other cooking equipment? According to the National Retail Federation, January is the best month to buy.

- When painting walls, look into easy methods like sponge painting or stenciling. There are many books that will make these techniques easy for even the clumsiest decorator. They you can use cheaper paint for the big areas, and more expensive paints as accents.

- Another intriguing, low-budged approach that will help you give that room a great new look: wallpaper borders. Not too expensive, but they can offer dramatically different effects. They're easy to change later on, too.

- Decorating with sheets is probably one of the best new decorating trends to develop over the past few years. There are a lot of books on the subject and at least once a year a few of the home-decorating magazines have complete directions on how to use sheets to make everything from curtains and slipcovers to pillows, tablecloths, and placemats. For more information, see *Singer Sewing for the Home* or *Fabric Magic* by Melanie Paine.

- And if you're going to be cutting sheets up and developing sewing projects around them, why not look into seconds? These manufacturer rejects, which usually have only minor cosmetic errors, are perfect for such projects; they can be bought at many discount houses. You may be able to save up to 50 percent. Call the Wamsutta/Springmaid factory outlets (615-756-0805) in Chattanooga, Tennessee. They're very helpful; if you know the name of the pattern you want, they'll help you track it down. You may also want to try the Fieldcrest/Cannon Factory Outlet Store: 800-841-3336 for Fieldcrest products, and 800-237-3209 for Cannon products. (P.S.: You can also bet bath rugs, towels, and comforters through these outlets!)

■ Bear in mind that plain sheets are almost always less expensive then patterns. Mixing these plain sheets in various combinations of tones and colors can make for some interesting looks. You can also dye white sheets to suit your color scheme.

■ Forget the expensive sheets by this year's name designers. You my find them next year in the bargain bin at your favorite discount store.

■ Do you have any old sheets at home that have worn edges or tears? Why not cut them up and use what fabric you can as accent trim or as throw pillows for larger projects?

■ Look for fabric in other unlikely places, too. Tablecloths and other old lines can be found at lots of flea markets and auctions (or, better yet, Mom's **attic**). You can often pick these up in large bundles rather then individually. Not all of the pieces will be great, and some may be stained, but cutting them up and patchworking them with other fabrics may give you a creative new look. Take the good pieces without stains and use them as they are, or as valances for curtains, or as tree skirts at Christmastime, or, if they're large enough, as covers for folding chairs.

■ If you've taken on a really big project, such as drapes for multiple windows, look into buying your fabric in quantity, by the bolt. Try a less expensive fabric like muslin. Experiment with wrapping the material loosely around a curtain rod, with the fabric pooling on the floor. Or make simple curtains, cut and trimmed to fit the windows and attached by plain ties to the rod.

■ Beware: Curtain rods can be prohibitively expensive! Depending on the length and the number of windows, you may have other options. If you have one rather large window to cover, consider using a plain wooden dowel from one of those huge warehouse hardware stores as a rod. If this window is the centerpiece of the room, how about a copper pipe or other metal pipe? You can add brass rings as sliders. Or try an uncut wooden closet rod. You can find these at lengths varying from standard to humongous at the larger hardware stores; they can be cut to fit any window. Stain the rod plain or paint it a wild color to add panache to plain fabric curtains.

■ Don't like any of those ideas when it comes to hanging a curtain? Take the real back-to-basics approach: track down a real branch. If you've (legal!) access to some woods, cut a small thin sapling or trim off a fairly even branch. You can either strip off the bark or leave it as is. Let the branch dry out in a cool, dry place for a few months to make sure it's not leaking any sap. When the branch is ready, seal it with a clear coat of polyurethane, or spraypaint it gold or silver.

■ Feeling in an artistic mood? Be ready to take advantage of a great find that will fit your (broad!) theme. If there's a sale on a brand of paint you like, you'll know what colors to be looking for from that point onward.

■ How about the Zen approach to decorating? Simple: very little furniture, white walls, simple white shades, walls left bare, room kept very clean. Warning: This scheme does not lend itself to homes with small children. It both is, and is not, a style. And you might just attain enlightenment if you sit there quietly for a few years. Ommm...

■ Then there's the Artist Look. Hang an old car fender on the wall—the more paint missing and the more rust present, the better. Call it sculpture. Hang an old drop cloth over a worn upholstered chair à la Jackson Pollock. Borrow a slide projector from your library; try your hand at wall murals. You paint on top of the image. Make sure your image projects evenly onto the wall, otherwise you'll have distortion. Consider continuing murals right over an old piece of furniture or door, as if they weren't there. The illusion will be impressively aesthetic. (Warning: Landlords may take a dim view of such adventures. Call first and go over what you have planned.)

■ Or you might prefer faux French Provincial. Paint old furniture white; accent it with gold paint and touches of light blue. Add inexpensive blue and white china vases and the knickknacks you can often find at discount houses. Use lots of candles in cheap holders (you can paint them gold, too), and don't forget to use lots of mirrors. You can find them at flea markets and yard sales. Feeling ambitious? This would be a good place to collaborate with your friendly neighborhood slide projector on a pastoral wall mural.

■ Want a Ralph Lauren–ish look? This really translates to a few simple elements: lots of bric-a-brac from Grandma's; lots of flannel; lots of plaid; lots of shelves cluttered with old cameras from the twenties, chess pieces, and obsolete writing implements. Affix snowshoes and old cross-country skis on the walls. Place this year's Currier and Ives calendar in an old unfinished frame. Toss a plaid throw blanket on the arm of a chair. Keep your colors rich and warm: deep red, black, forest green. Add lots of wood. Let room cool; serve with hot chocolate while discussing F. Scott Fitzgerald.

■ Before you pay money for someone else's decorating advice, remember that the place you live in is *your* sanctuary. Surround yourself with things you love, and forget any rules about decorating you may have been taught. The only rule that counts is to make sure you like the place.

■ Bare-living-room syndrome? Instead of buying that hefty new piece of furniture at a hefty price, check out local yard sales for pieces waiting to be rescued from years of hideous overpainting. There's often a striking piece of hardwood furniture waiting to be discovered underneath all the gunk.

■ If you're arranging flowers, a large raw potato may be just what you need for a base. Cut it in half; place the flat side down. Poke some holes with an ice pick, and insert the stems in the holes. Cover the potato with an attractive patterned cloth.

■ Well-placed large flowering plants (such as lilacs, forsythia, and wisteria) can provide shade for the hot spots in your house. Placing these appropriately can make your place look great *and* helps cut down on your cooling bills during the summer months. Each of these plants can be bought when small for under $10. They grow relatively quickly, too.

Cleaning

Scrub-a-dub-dub: Here are loads of thrifty ideas that will help you keep your abode spotless.

■ Cleaning carpets? Use the cheapest (foaming) shaving

cream you can find. Spray it on, then rinse with dampened towels. Go easy on the foam, though. You don't want to get the base of the carpet wet.

■ Don't toss that bedraggled old toothbrush! It's one of the best cleaning tools your home will ever meet. It will help you scrub out all those hard-to-reach areas that nothing else can get to.

■ Ever wonder how to clean your can opener? Try scrubbing it with a toothbrush. Rinse well, then spray the working pieces with nonstick vegetable spray as a natural lubricant. Next time, it will clean up even easier.

■ Natural Kitchen Deodorizer Department: If you have a lemon or orange that's past its prime, cut it in half and throw it down the garbage disposal. Smells great!

■ Cleaning products are expensive. Consider buying them in larger professional concentrates. Look for these first in your local buyer's guide—ask a librarian for help. Or check the yellow pages for a local cleaning company and ask what *they* use. These products are concentrates and should, as a general rule, be diluted for home use in reusable spray bottles or other small containers. Follow the label directions. Store concentrates in basement or garage, out of the reach of children.

■ Diluting cleaners with less water "so they'll work better" is almost always a waste of money. There's virtually never any noticeable improvement in the results.

■ Back-to-Basics Department: Good old ammonia may be the most effective all-purpose cleaner out there. There's not much it can't overcome, although the scent is strong enough to choke a horse. (Fortunately, it does come in scented versions nowadays.) Dilute with water, following the directions on the label, and open the windows. Think it's too much? To each his own, but let me ask you this: When was the last time you wiped out a diaper pail? Never, never, never combine ammonia with bleach. They call that concoction mustard gas. It was all too effective in World War I.

■ Streaky panes? Mix 1 ounce of ammonia with 2 ounces of rubbing alcohol, 1/4 teaspoon of dishwashing detergent, and a pint of water. Now you have a window cleaner that will not only clean well, but will prevent frost on your car windows!

■ Bad stain in the bathroom tub or sink? Try a mixture of hydrogen peroxide and cream of tartar. Get out that old toothbrush, scrub, and rinse well. If the stain is still there, and it may very well be, try again, only this time add a few drops of ammonia. Let stand a few hours and then scrub. Still no luck? Sad to say, some of the more stubborn stains in the bathroom fall into the "re-enamel me or get used to it" category. Have you considered installing a nice red light bulb for that retro sixties look? Stains disappear like magic—and you can develop film, too!

■ For *small* scuff and black marks on floors, try scrubbing with peanut butter or toothpaste. No, I'm not kidding. Using these overlooked gentle abrasives is a better bet than buying a whole bottle of some specialized cleaner. (But note that this method is not cost-effective for larger stains.)

■ Believe-It-or-Not Department, continued: Toothpaste also makes a perfectly appropriate gentle abrasive cleaner for that ground-in dirt on your kids' elbows and knees. They'll giggle all through the scrub! Don't dry this if they've got cuts or sores in those areas, though.

- Scuff marks on walls? Paint over them. Use a primer coat, the repaint the scuff area with paint left over from the original paint job. You did save some, right? If not, buy the smallest amount possible and keep it on hand—even if you only have enough to fill baby food jars. Trust me, even this small amount will go a long way. It also makes sense to keep a quart of primer on hand.

- To make wall cleaning easier, always paint walls with semigloss paints.

- The next time you paint, track down a brand-new wooden paint stirrer (you know, the kind they give away when you buy the paint). Dip it into freshly stirred paint. Then, after it dries, repeat the process for the second coat. When the stirrer dries, write the name of the paint and the brand, as well as any catalog number you can find, in pen on an unpainted area. Hang the stirrer inside your paint closet. The next time you need to match your paint color, you'll have all the information you need—plus a paint sample large enough to scan at the paint store. Beats buying a half gallon of the wrong stuff, doesn't it?

- Remember, nothing says clean—or not-so-clean—like the *smell* of your house. The very best (and cheapest) treatment for this is something I like to call fresh air. Open the windows often and give our house a good airing.

- My grandmother always said there was nothing the sun couldn't clean. Guess what? She was right! After washing delicate fabrics, hanging them out in bright sun to dry will gently bleach out many stains. Do check that weather report beforehand, though.

- Heres a quilter's trick. If you prick your finger and get a blood stain on fabric, immediately dab an ice cube directly onto the stain. Continue dabbing as the ice melts; this will draw out the blood and wash it away at the same time. If this doesn't work the first time, try running the fabric under very cold water, then turning the piece over and repeating the process on the other side. Remember, hot water will set a stain.

■ Take some of your old clothes, the ones you're not going to give to the Goodwill people, and tear them into dust rags. Lightly spray them with water and dust away. When they need washing, put them in with your towels and dry using fabric softeners. (And see the advice on fabric softeners below.) This will keep them picking up dirt for you.

■ Who needs store-bought fabric softener? Try putting a drop or two of hair conditioner on a dry or wet washcloth and throwing it into the dryer. You'll never notice the difference, and it will smell good, too.

■ Okay, okay, you like using fabric softener sheets. (Me, I find that cuddly teddy bear a little scary, but it takes all kinds.) Always use the dryer sheets twice. Who can tell the difference?

■ Never use more detergent then recommended. Sometimes even a little less works just as well if the load is light or the wash is not too dirty. More is never better when it comes to cleaners.

■ Do you, like me, hate cleaning house? Don't pay someone to come and do it for you. Rock out and have a little fun. Play your favorite song loud, and dance enthusiastically while you clean. Sure, leave the windows open. What's the worst thing your neighbors can say? "Oh, there goes Leslie with the Beatles music, she must be cleaning again." It works for me. Plus, if you dance while you work, you'll burn off some of those pesky calories.

- Here's another cleaning trick that's infinitely prèferable to hiring someone to do your dirty work. Pretend someone famous is coming over at the last minute. Just pretend that Harrison Ford, say, has just called and informed you that he is on his way. You only have twenty minutes to pick up the house. Go! Then, when the job is done, put one of his movies on the VCR and sit back to relax in your clean house. It works for men, too. Maybe Winona Ryder?

- More from the Back-to-Basics Grab Bag: Borax is a highly effective old-fashioned cleaner; whenever I smell it, it reminds me of Grandma's. She was a sharp women who knew the advantage of using a cleaner with more then one purpose. Today, you can find boron in cleaners like Borax, Boraxo, and others. In the laundry, it acts as a booster to your everyday laundry detergent. Borax can often be used as a substitute for dish detergent! But read the directions on your box first to make sure your brand doesn't include any harsh chemicals.

- Odor problems in the kitchen or bathroom? Not if you've got an orange and a container of salt around. Take an orange half and hollow it out, removing the pulp. Then pour some salt in the hollow and start scrubbing. This is quite effective at removing even the strongest of odors— and leaving behind the light scent of oranges. When you're done, toss the orange rind down your garbage disposal; it will refresh things there, too.

- Strange smells issuing from the garbage disposal? Before you call the plumber, pour half a cup of salt down your garbage disposal. More often than not, the problem will vanish.

- Ever wonder what they used to clean copper pots before someone invented those expensive chemical preparations?

Add 1/2 teaspoon salt to 1/4 cup vinegar, and you've got the perfect abrasive for your copper pots. Combine with little elbow grease (you needed a little toning and strengthening anyway, right?) and you'll have the brightest, shiniest pots in town. No toxic, otherworldly odor, either.

- Another inexpensive, low-tech method for cleaning copper pots: half a lemon with a couple of teaspoons of salt sprinkled on the surface. Rub.

- Instead of coughing up four bucks for a special bathroom-fixture cleaner, pour some vinegar into a paper towel. Your chromium faucets will sparkle like new.

- To get rid of mildew on the inside of your refrigerator, wipe it down occasionally with vinegar. It will get things so clean, you may even venture into the vegetable drawer on a more regular basis.

- Looking for a way to remove lime deposits from the bottom of your tea kettle—without paying for expensive cleaning preparations? Try filling the pot with equal parts water and vinegar. Boil for about ten to fifteen minutes; let it stand overnight. Give the kettle a good shake, pour out the water, then rinse. Repeat as necessary.

- You can get great results from the least expensive dishwashing detergent available. Just add a few tablespoons of vinegar to the dishwasher. The vinegar will cut the grease—and your dishes will sparkle.

- Have you read the side of a baking soda box recently? I think anything you can digest *and* clean with is truly amazing. Believe it or not, baking soda is often the *only* active ingredient in many modern cleansers. (It's also the new hip thing to clean your teeth with, just like it was fifty or sixty years ago!) You already know that baking soda works great as deodorizer for the refrigerator, but did you know it's also a carpet freshener? Just sprinkle some on a dry rug, leave on for about an hour, and vacuum. The room will be free of odor. The baking soda gets rid of the smells you wanted gone, and it doesn't leave behind a cover-up odor like overdone potpourri or industrial-strength, reconstituted, chemical forest scent.

- Because baking soda leaves no odor behind, it also works great for cleaning thermoses and coffeepots. Just wash normally, giving the item a little scrub and rinsing. They'll last longer, too.

- Skip the soft-scrub cleansers; you can use baking soda as a mild abrasive on countertops and pots and pans.

- Baking soda also works well when you need to remove greasy buildup from any knickknack that sits around the stovetop a lot: salt and pepper shakers, vases, that kind of thing.

- The good people at Arm and Hammer can give you lots more information on the many ways you can use baking soda as a safe, inexpensive cleanser. Write them at Box 4533, Department E, Monticello, MN 55365, for information.

- Here's another low-cost, low-tech method for keeping your fridge odor-free: a piece of cotton dipped in vanilla extract. (Mmm...)

- If odor problems are persistent, don't toss out the refrigerator and head to Sears for another one. Try placing a small bowl of charcoal (the kind found at plant stores) in a back corner of the refrigerator.

- While we're on the subject of refrigerators, have you been wondering whether there is an easier way to clean underneath the thing than moving the whole fridge away from the wall? Save that sacroiliac, and don't put that slipped disc to the test any more than you have to. Tie a sock or two onto the end of a yardstick. Dip the socks in an ammonia-and-water solution; clean away.

■ Dust the coils on the back of your refrigerator every month or two; you'll keep your machine running more efficiently and hence more economically.

■ Simple cornstarch has been shown to be a *safer* choice for babies than expensive talcum powder preparations. Why pay more for the brand that has that "powdery" smell? The baby doesn't care about perfume. Just for the record, I happen to think babies smell great just the way they are. Most of the time.

■ Try sprinkling some cornstarch on your furniture after you've polished it. It will absorb any excess oil, making your furniture shine longer.

■ Got a grease stain on a piece of clothing or upholstery? Quick. Grab some cornstarch and apply it to whatever got accidentally gooped. Let the fabric dry and brush it off. If you act quickly, you'll stand a pretty good chance of removing the stain completely.

■ Shred a bunch of old newspapers and dampen them. Then toss the pieces around the bare floor of the room you're cleaning. I know this sounds like *making* a mess, not cleaning one, but wait. If you're trying to clean up pet hair, this simple method works great. Simply sweep up the paper, it collects the dust and hair as you go. Scoop it up and throw it away. (By the way, the newspaper is still recyclable!) Beats calling a professional cleaner, right?

Repairing, Protecting, and Maintaining Your Home

You live there, right? So why not take a few frugal steps to keep your place looking great—or even improve things a bit? You never know when the in-laws are going to drop by unexpectedly.

■ Take on only those projects you feel quite comfortable doing yourself. You can make a simple job much more expensive in the long run if your "improvements" result in major repairs afterward. In addition, be sure you take all appropriate safety measures. Hospitals are expensive, too.

■ Ask a friend or relative to help you out on a job they've done themselves. (Helpful quality-control hint: During a visit at the friend or relative's home, check out just how well the job really came out. No sense inviting Aunt Hortense over to screw up your house, too.)

■ Electric blankets are frowned upon by fire personnel and insurance adjusters. Go with a couple of strategically placed hot-water bottles instead. Put them in about half an hour before you plan to go to sleep.

■ Ever notice that the hand-pumped soap that comes out of those dispensers you buy is awfully thick? I cut mine with an equal amount of water and store the remainder for later use. Cheaper, of course, but I actually prefer the consistency.

■ Those magazines you're subscribing to—and allowing to take over your home—are available for *free* review at your local library. Just a thought: Canceling your subscriptions and making more regular pilgrimages to the library could be the way to go. What about that article you *have* to post on the refrigerator? Hey, that's what God made photo-copiers for, right?

■ You may be able to save 12,000 gallons of water annually

by replacing your showerhead with a low-flow one. This can save as much as $75 a year in water and sewer charges.

■ Negotiating substantial home repairs with a contractor? These can be a pain in the pocketbook, but you can lessen the pain if you offer to hold an open house in your home after the work is done—in return for a discount. Don't sign anything until you've tried this!

■ Thinking of cosmetic or relatively minor repairs? If your friends and family members are home owners who also need home improvements, why not simply gather your resources and help each other out when it comes to jobs that you can't accomplish on your own? With a good-sized work crew, you can get a room painted fast. The same goes for sanding, wallpapering, yard work, and more. But remember, the person whose house gets the group treatment has to spring for pizza.

■ Keeping shrubs neatly trimmed around the house is an excellent way to keep would-be burglars from lurking about. You'll provide both neighbors and police with a clear view of your property.

■ Motion-sensor outdoor lights are a thrifty way to protect the valuables inside your home—they're usually a good deal less expensive than elaborate timing systems, and if you set them up properly, they're just about as effective. These lights only turn on when something moves outside; it's as though someone inside flipped the switch after hearing something rustle oddly. (The light stays on for a short time, then switches itself off until the motion detector is activated again.) These lights turn on when *anything* moves: branches in the wind and curious squirrels, as well as ax-wielding maniacs. You can get one for around twelve bucks. The light, that is. Not the ax-wielding maniac.

- Looking for a cheap and effective lawn treatment? Washing your car on your lawn can be good for it. The grass may actually do better by being exposed to your detergents, and highly acidic soil may improve as a result of a (judicious) soap-down. Don't waste water, though.

- The most important content in fertilizer is nitrogen. The brand that contains the most for the least money is the best brand to buy.

- Buy a push mower. You can often find these at bargain prices at yard sales. Sharpen the blades yourself with a hand file. You'd be surprised how well an oiled and sharpened push mower will work. It's noise-free, pollution-free, gas-free, and you virtually never have to repair the thing. You'll also get a great workout, which was on your list anyway, right?

- Buy grass seeds that are indigenous to the region. Grass made to grow lush in southern California will never grow as well in Vermont. Ask at your garden center for seeds that grow well in your area and under your conditions: shady, sunny, or a combination of the two.

- Don't get too wrapped up in the perfect lawn. It's not supposed to be a lush carpet of bright green. Sure, with enough chemicals, you can make it one, but at what cost to you and your environment? Those lawn treatment companies put up little signs that say not to walk on it—or to let your pets walk on it—because it may cause burns. Does that really sound like something you want to have around the people and animals you love?

- I'm one of those people who is always cold. I lived in Hawaii; I was cold there, too. Now I live back home in New England, and I have learned to make use of a sweater, some warm fuzzy slippers, and an oversized flannel nightgown. Every once in a while, I may look a little weird, but my heating bills don't.

- It's no fun to lose a favorite garment because of dark colors that run in the washing machine. Sort your laundry carefully.

- Apartment dwellers: Here's a no-cost way to improve your living standards (and avoid the expensive hospital bills so often associated with nearly freezing to death). Remind your landlord that hot water radiators must be bled periodically for maximum heat efficiency. If he or she doesn't take the hint, call the appropriate state regulatory agency and complain until something happens.

- Are you really watching that premium cable channel you're paying $9.95 a month for? If so, how often?

- Barter with friends and neighbors to get home-repair-related supplies you need. In return for letting your neighbor use your snowblower, ask to borrow his mulcher.

- Before you load your dishwasher, wipe the dishes or rinse them briefly with cool water. This can save you over $100 a year—and you'll be saved the aggravation of finding crusty dishes in the "clean" load!

- Boil water by covering the pot. It's quicker and will use less energy.

- Buying a large quantity of something at retail? Ask to see the manager before you hand over your credit card. Ask for a quantity discount, Often, you'll receive it.

■ Check in at your local hardware store; it may offer free do-it-yourself seminars.

■ Check the Energyguide sticker closely before purchasing any major appliance. This will summarize the estimated yearly energy costs you can expect when using the appliance.

■ Concerned about your electric bills? The Department of Energy recommends that you consider switching to compact fluorescent lamps, which use about 75 percent less energy than incandescent lamps. (They also emit 90 percent less heat while giving off the same amount of light, which is a plus during the summer months.) Ask about compact fluorescent lamps at your local hardware store.

■ Confused by some of the terminology you're hearing during the home-buying process? Ask Uncle Sam for a little help. Write the U.S. Department of Housing and Urban Development and ask for a copy of their helpful pamphlet, *Home Buyer's Terminology*. It will set you straight on the most important terms—and maybe save you some bucks when negotiating time comes around. It always helps to know what you're paying for, right?

■ Consider getting a "set-back" thermostat, one that automatically turns the heat down when you go to bed, up just before your get up, down just after you leave for work, and back up before you get home. If you rent, ask your landlord about this option. If you own your own home, call a couple of heating contractors for estimates on the prices involved.

■ Do you have access to a pickup truck? Use it to pick up

your own furniture or appliance purchases. You'll save on delivery charges and get a little exercise, too.

■ Does your house seem like an oven during summertime? There are alternatives to cranking up the AC. Painting the house, for instance. According to the Department of Energy, "Dull, dark-colored home exteriors absorb 70 percent to 90 percent of the radiant energy that strikes the home's surfaces. Some of this absorbed energy is then transferred into your home by way of conduction, resulting in heat gain." That's a good thing if your aim is to keep the home toasty during wintertime, but if keeping things cool during the summer is a higher priority, you might want to think about picking a lighter shade for your home the next time it needs a new coat.

■ During the summer months, try not to run major appliances during the daytime. You'll keep the house cooler, rely on the air conditioner less, and help keep electrical demand down during peak hours. Don't turn the fridge off, though. The ice cream will melt.

■ Have your oil burner tuned up regularly by a trained professional. Winter will be warmer, and less expensive, if you do. The better heating-oil supply companies offer economical maintenance programs you can take advantage of.

■ Here's a simple two-way measure you can take that will help keep you warm in the winter and cool in the summer: weatherization. Write the Department of Energy at 1000 Independence Avenue, SW, Washington, DC 20585, and ask for the fact sheet *Insulation*.

■ Here's one way to cool things down during summertime: Hang light-colored curtains. Draperies made of fabric that is woven tightly, light in hue, and opaque do a better job of reflecting sunlight. Sunlight that doesn't get into your house can't make it feel like a sauna.

■ How about getting your utility company to write you a check for a change? The Department of Energy points out that "many utility companies offer rebates and other cost incentives when you purchase or install energy-saving products." Call your local utility and ask if they're planning to pay you to buy something you were going to get anyway.

■ If you're planting trellises near your home, the Department of Energy recommends that you set them some distance away from the house. This way, air will be able to circulate freely around the building, a real plus during the summer months. In addition, you'll keep the plants from attaching themselves to the outside of your home and damaging the exterior.

■ If you heat your home with gas, bear in mind that this system should be checked for efficiency every two years or so. Call your gas company for details.

■ If your home has radiators, think about installing reflectors made of nonflammable material. These work by reflecting heat away from the wall and back into the room.

■ If your steam radiator is releasing steam and not hot air, you've got a problem. Call your landlord or a qualified repair person to make sure your apartment is being heated at maximum efficiency during the winter months.

■ Is your water heater working harder than it has to? Try setting it at a lower level and see if the system still delivers satisfactory results for your home.

■ Keep closet doors shut and seal off unused rooms during winter. Heat only the rooms you're using.

- Looking for more information on the best ways to lower your energy bills? Write the Energy Efficiency and Renewable Energy Clearinghouse, P.O. Box 3048, Merrifield, VA 22116, and ask to see a list of their publications. This organization provides free general and technical information on many energy-related topics.

- Looking to buy a house? Take advantage of home-buying seminars; you'll learn how to save big-time. Check with your local housing authority for details.

- Need a clothes dryer? Check the classifieds for used machines before buying a new one. Dryers have very few moving parts; it's hard to go wrong with a used machine in fairly good shape.

- Passive solar design and construction may be able to help you cut your utility bills. To find out more about how current technologies could streamline your next renovation or building project, write the Passive Solar Industries Council (PSIC), at 1511 K Street, NW, Suite 600, Washington, DC 20005, or call them at 202-628-7400.

- Planting trees around the house? Think of the energy implications before you do. The Department of Energy recommends that you plant trees on the northeast-southwest and northwest-southwest sides of your home—and avoid planting trees directly to the south unless you live in a climate that is warm year-round. Following these steps will help keep your home cool in the summer. Leaving the southern portion of the house unobstructed will help keep things warm in the winter.

- Remember to close the damper on your fireplace when you're done using it. Heat does rise, after all, and there's no sense warming up the great outdoors!

- Reuse plastic grocery bags to line your small garbage baskets.

- Seal (or have your landlord seal) leaky doors with caulk for maximum heating efficiency during the winter months. Make sure the doors still open after the project is complete.

- Some people find that their dishes come out just as clean when the dishwasher is placed on the "cold" or "economy" setting. If this works for you, you may be able to realize substantial savings on your heating bill.

- Washers, dryers, dishwashers, and water heaters can generate a whole lot of heat and humidity, which can make things unbearable during summertime. If possible, seal off your laundry room and water heater from the rest of the house.

- When you go to bed at night, and when you're out of the house, turn your thermostat to 55 degrees. You'll save on your winter heating bills. (Note: This is not recommended for people with circulatory problems or other medical issues!)

- Mulch your leaves by either using a mulching mower or borrowing a shredder from a friend. (Be careful here; follow all the appropriate safety procedures.) When your leaves have been chopped into a smaller size, rake them into a pile. Turn them often, and you've got a great start at your own compost pile. I use mine piled around my roses to protect their roots over the winter.

Alternate Approaches: Finding a Place to Live

Suppose you haven't found the perfect house or apartment yet. Other than checking the want ads, are there any unconventional ways you can track down the best housing for your situation? Here are some ideas.

- Looking for a roommate? One of the best (commission-free!) ways to find one is to post a bold, full-color notice on your local church or synagogue's bulletin board—or write up a snappy notice for the weekly bulletin. Both options are free, and the candidates who respond are more likely to share your worldview and some of your interests than people answering classified ads.

- Use Internet's regional-housing bulletin-board discussion groups to help you find the best values appropriate to your situation. Just post an electronic note outlining what you're looking for, and see what comes back. Here is a list of the relevant major boards as of this writing; all are easily accessible through the Usenet portion of the Internet. Alas, not all areas blessed with a regional-housing-related board; the list below represents the best information available at press time. (Check with your on-line service provider for advice on the best ways to access the Usenet function and post to these boards or others that may help you resolve questions. For California (San Francisco Bay Area): ba.housing • For California (San Diego area): sdnet.housing • For the District of Columbia: dc.housing • For New England (Massachusetts, New Hampshire, Connecticut, Maine, Rhode Island, Vermont):ne.housing • For New Jersey: nj.housing • For New York/New Jersey/Connecticut (Tri-state area/Greater New York City area): nyc.market.housing • For Washington State (Seattle area): seattle.forsale.housing

- Feel like bettering the odds of finding the perfect abode during your trip through cyberspace? Post a note on the general-interest regional Usenet boards in your area, too.

(There are a lot more of them.) See the full list in the "Vacations and Travel" chapter of this book.

■ Interested in a more creative approach to the whole housing issue? There *are* alternatives to traditional home-buying arrangements. Find out about cohousing, a shared-living philosophy that focuses on the development of linked single-family dwellings with central cooking and utility areas, and the common development of a safe, secure living environment by neighbors/co-owners. This has been big in Denmark for years. To learn more about cohousing efforts in your area, send $6 to Rob Sandlin, 22020 East Lost Lake Road, Snohomish, WA 98290, and ask for a copy of the *The Cohousing Resource Guide*. Online go to COHOUSING-L (your first name) (your last name) to listserv@uci.com, you'll get the latest notes and ideas about this fascinating topic—for free!

■ Low-income applicants may be eligible for loans from the Farmers Home Administration to purchase or repair a home located on a farm or in a very rural area. For more information, write to Farmers Home Administration, Department of Agriculture, Washington, DC 20250.

■ Low-income families who rent their homes may be eligible for housing assistance payments from the U.S. Department of Housing and Urban Development. For information on eligibility for rent assistance programs, write the U.S. Department of Housing and Urban Development, 451 Seventh Street SW, Washington, DC 20410.

3

Cars

Almost everybody needs a car. If you don't, consider yourself lucky. Cars are a pain. You have to park them. You have to insure them. You have to worry about birds leaving gifts on them. To me, it's amazing how badly we all wanted one as a teenager. If we had known what a tremendous hassle they were we would never have bothered. Anyway, if you're like most people, you need a car to get where you want to go. Fortunately, you probably don't have to spend as much as you think.

Just a Question Before We Begin

And one worth pondering before you put down your hard-earned cash, too: Do you need a car in the first place? For many people (most notably city-dwellers), a transit pass is a much more convenient alternative. No parking hassles, no tickets, no insurance problems, no garage fees—and you're doing the environment a favor, too.

Buying a Used Car

No, it's not a cop-out option. Read on.

- Why *not* consider this first? As soon as you drive a new car off the lot, it depreciates by 10 percent. From a dollar-value standpoint, buying a used car is often a very smart move. Remember, *used* doesn't have to mean all that *old*. Sometimes you'll be able to track down a vehicle that suits all your needs perfectly, is only a year or two old, and has many (if not all) the same features as the new model. A car that's a few years old has depreciated but lost very little mechanical life. You can often save thousands of dollars on an excellent vehicle with warranties still valid.

- Consider a junker. No kidding; if you're mechanically inclined, this may be the very best value...and a stimulating source of ongoing technical challenge, as well! Seriously, a car you don't particularly love frees you. You don't have to spend your weekends waxing it to a high sheen. You drive it for the simple reason that it gets you were you want to go. (Like *that* counts for anything.) And when you're battling with a Mercedes for a prime merging position, who do you think is going to come out ahead? Park the junker a block away from where you live and keep it in safe driving condition, either on your own or through the good offices of a mechanic who happens to be a blood relative.

- If you do purchase a junker for the above-mentioned reasons, be sure that either you or someone you love has an aptitude and an interest in repairing it. This option works best for those who have made car maintenance an ongoing hobby, or who knows someone who has done so. For the rest of us mere mortals, the garage costs can quickly wipe out any savings. What you're looking for is something that may need occasional tender loving care, but that will run dependably once that has been administered.

- When checking out a used car, take the time to look closely at the tires. These can often offer clues to trouble elsewhere in the vehicle. Uneven tread wear can be a sign of previous accidents or of improper alignment. You could also be looking at a serious suspension problem.

- Buying a used *rental* vehicle from a responsible national or regional chain may be the best route to a quality used car purchase. The maintenance on these vehicles is usually impeccable, and you will usually be able to inspect exhaustive written records reflecting each car's maintenance and repair history.

- Always have a used car checked out by a trusted mechanic before you sign the check. It's not that the vehicle has to be *perfect*, of course, but there's no sense in buying a corpse, right?

- Before you buy a used car, don't forget to check for a spare tire and all the tire-changing equipment. If this stuff doesn't come with the vehicle and the seller can't or won't provide the equipment, demand a lower price.

Buying a New Car

- Before you buy that new car, review the previous section on buying a *used* car. Are you absolutely sure that you need this expense right now? If so, here are some tips you'll find helpful.

- Buying a new car is, almost by definition, an emotional choice. That's okay—but try to make your "personal statement" in terms of externals like color and accessories as opposed to the model of the car.

- Identify what you really need from the car; isolate three or four top candidates that will probably get the job done for you. What are you going to be hauling around? What kind of gas mileage are you looking for? What kind of maintenance do you expect to perform or pay for? Once you've narrowed your search down, do some homework on the top candidates. Get yourself a copy of the dealer's invoice or factory invoice . . . but not from the dealer! You can have the newest, most recently updated prices and rebate information faxed to you directly from *Consumer Reports* magazine's New Car Prices Services (800-395-4400) for a fee of $12. Considering that the information you receive is likely to save you hundreds (if not thousands!) of dollars, it will be money very well spent.

■ You may also want to consult *Edmund's New Car Prices.* Ask for a copy of the most recent edition at your local library.

■ Add the invoice price, destination charges, and any additional options you want, then subtract rebates. Now you know exactly how much you'll be spending. (The dealer's cubicle is not the place to decide how much you want to pay.) After you've done your math, determine exactly how much you are willing to pay over the dealer cost. Knowing this figure—and refusing to deviate from it—will put you at a significant advantage during the negotiation phase.

■ With the *Consumer Reports* printout in hand, and knowing your absolute upper limit, walk into that dealer's cubicle and get ready to haggle. When in doubt, wave your *Consumer Reports* printout in the salesperson's face. Smile. Even at so-called no-haggle establishments, you can still expect to save anywhere from 2 to 4 percent.

■ If the salesperson offers a "provisional yes" to your price, but says that he has to take the numbers to his boss and have them "approved," don't get flustered. There may not be any boss approving anything. The salesperson may just be making coffee and checking his hair. (See if he doesn't come back with neater hair. It should be your clue.) Be willing at any moment to shake hands and walk away. There is always a better deal somewhere else. And anyway, dealers just hate it when customers smile and say they'll try someplace else. (You'll feel great doing it, too.)

- If you live in a small town with only one car dealership, *don't shop there.* Go to a bigger town with lots of other dealerships nearby. Take advantage of the competition.

- Write your state attorney general's office or office of consumer affairs for information on your state's "lemon laws." If someone sells you a clunker, you may have important legal options to consider.

Repairing It

Drat! It won't go, and you can't find the magic wand. Oh, well. Here are some suggestions on getting repair work down economically.

- The first rule of fixing a car yourself is knowing when you're looking at a job that only a professional should take on. For most of us, transmission and electrical problems, for instance, are great reasons to call that uncle who runs a repair shop. Know your limitations—and don't take any chances when it comes to safety. That having been said, read on.

- Parts bought at car parts shops are always cheaper than those bought at the dealership. You can often find small garages that will put them in for you, charging you only for their labor.

- Parts for used cars can often be found in auto junkyards. If you're ready to pull that piece out of the dead version of your car and patch it into yours, you can often get the parts you need to get your car running—for next to nothing. I call this the Frankenstein method of car upkeep.

■ When practicing the Frankenstein method, remember that the part you take out of the junked car may not be a working part. This seems obvious, I know, but the principle takes on grave importance when dealing with critical parts: brakes, say, rather than windshield wipers. When in doubt, ask a professional.

■ Be prepared to do some horse trading with the junkyard proprietor. Sometimes they'll give you a better price of you bargain for the whole front grille, rather than the single headlight you need. If you take it off the lot yourself, that is.

Cleaning, Maintaining, and Everyday Use

Sometimes you can impress people just as much with a clean *old* car as someone else does with a yucky *new* one. Here are some ideas for keeping it clean and running smooth from bumper to bumper...on a budget.

■ Avoid expensive body repair bills. Wash your car every month, even in the winter. Road salt and sand can do a lot of damage, both on the outside and to the interior of your car. Make sure you get down on hands and knees and rinse the underside of your car, too—that's where much of the rust starts.

■ Here's a thrifty recipe for homemade windshield wiper fluid: a gallon of water, a couple of drops of dishwashing liquid, and a pint of rubbing alcohol. It works—and you don't have to drive anywhere in a hailstorm to get it.

- Do you honestly need a car phone? If you drive a lot at night, alone, there may be a safety argument. It's nice to be able to call a tow truck without leaving the vehicle. Otherwise, you might as well save your money.

- If you're driving a car that you think may be affected by a recent recall notice, but aren't certain about your vehicle's status, don't chance it. Call the National Highway Traffic Safety Administration at 800-366-0123 and get all the details.

- Never risk getting a ticket—keep plenty of change in your car for parking meters. (But keep it in an inconspicuous spot; some people will break into an automobile on the flimsiest pretexts.)

- Post those discount oil-change coupons on your refrigerator. Everyone gets them these days; use them to remind yourself to take the car in for a scheduled visit. Usually the coupons really will save you a good deal of money—but be sure to read them carefully.

- If you buy a used child safety seat, check the underside of it. This will be touching your car's seats. If you see any rough spots, sand the area and coat with a primer or rust sealer until the surface is smooth. You'll avoid leaving scuff marks, and you won't have to replace or repair the upholstery quite so quickly as you otherwise might. This is one of the few kid-related stains you can prevent ahead of time.

- Alternate approach: Before you put that car seat in, put a plastic tarp (or a piece of shower curtain) down on the seat. This prevents scuffing—and it's much easier to clean than the upholstery.

- If you have to park in the sun, protect your leather of vinyl interior by shielding it. Forget that aluminized plastic shield some places are hawking, though. It's too expensive, and a sheet of cardboard is just as effective. Cut one yourself from an old box. (The venetian-blind fan style is almost completely ineffective, and it, too, costs way too much.)

- Use floor mats in the front *and back* of the car. They'll keep people's heels from digging into the upholstery and let you go longer between vacuumings. (Just remove the mats and shake them out.)

- Have the oil changed more often than the manual recommends. About every three thousand miles is probably your best bet. This the single most important (and maybe easiest) thing you can do to prolong the life of your car.

- Change your oil filter when your oil gets changed. With many cars, this is recommended every *other* time you change the oil—but considering the consequences, I say, for about $4 a filter, it's a job worth doing. Besides, what if you can't remember whether you changed it last time?

- While you're at it, rotate the tires. They'll last longer.

- Keep extensive records of all maintenance. This will help you later when it comes to troubleshooting during repair time, and it will make selling the vehicle a lot easier, too.

- Younger kids love to help clean the car. Enlist their help before they know they're doing something useful. Reward their fine efforts with a trip to the playground.

- Teenagers, by contrast, know that when you suggest that they clean the car, that means you want them to perform work of some kind. Tell them they can *use* the car only if they clean it once they return home or first thing the next morning. Reward their fine efforts by not helping. (You know how uncool it is to actually be seen doing something constructive with one's parents.)

- You know that "Hot Wax" light that goes on in the drive-through car wash, the one they charge a dollar to turn on? I don't think anything happens when you push it.

Selling It

You never thought the day would come—okay, maybe you did. Either way, you want to get the most you can for your beloved vehicle. Here are some ideas.

- Keeping your car garaged can add to its resale value. (And, of course, significantly reduce the likelihood of its being stolen.) If you've got no garage and don't feel like paying for one, then keep the vehicle covered as often as possible. The exterior of the car will hold up far better than it will if you leave it out to face the elements.

- Nothing makes an old car look better than a new paint job. The money you pay *may* add far more than that amount to the car's resale value. Shop around for the best rate, and don't be afraid to quote one shop's estimate for the benefit of another's.

- Ask whether the paint shop will charge you less if you remove all your own grillwork and mirrors (and anything else that won't be getting painted). You may get a much better price on the job—and you may also show your vehicle a little more T.L.C. during the removal and reassembly process than the staff would.

- Remember, the most popular color for a car is fire engine red. The car may sell faster if you paint it in a fast looking color like this one. The paint shop proprietor may be able to give you a deal on another color...because he might have a lot of it around. There may just be a reason for this. In my humble opinion, nothing looks good in avocado, not even refrigerators.

4

Food and Groceries

Attention shoppers: Your grocery bill is that portion of the monthly budget over which you have the most day-to-day control! Here are some ideas for getting the very most bang for your buck at the checkout counter.

- Stick to your list! Only make exceptions to take advantage of an unforeseen bargain in a category you would eventually buy in anyway. (No, marked-down cartons of imported yak sausages don't count.)

- Do some investigating, then pick one local market with good prices and stay with it to buy *most* of what you need. (But see the advice on bulk-purchase discount outlets below.) Running from one store to another to take advantage of every advertised sale may not be at all cost effective. If the stores aren't close together, the cost of gas alone could outweigh any savings. See the U.S. Department of Agriculture, Home and Garden Bulletin no. 183, *Your Money's Worth in Foods*.

- Don't be afraid to stop in at a bulk-discount outlet every once in a while. These no-frill stores may offer great bargains, but only in bulk. If you have the space to store all the stuff, consider making a stop for selected items. And speaking of space...

■ Start a pantry. This means a large, cool, dry space with enough room to store bulk items that will keep for a long time: paper towels, toilet paper, dry pasta, canned goods, things like that. By finding room for bulk items, you can save up to 30 percent. Don't think you have any storage room? Apartment dwellers have found some pretty inventive spaces for pantries, including discreetly blocked-off corners of the bedroom closet—or even beneath the bed! You might try setting up shelves in the laundry room (if you have one), over your washer and dryer. Homeowners may want to consider the garage—but remember to keep items in a storage closet to discourage any critters that might find paper towels a nice home for the winter.

■ Don't buy *perishables* in bulk unless you really will eat all of the item before it goes bad. In other words, beware of the wilted-lettuce syndrome. It's not pretty.

■ Lists are good. Lists can help you save money. But don't be a slave to them! You should, for instance, be ready to check the weekly specials in the meat department of the grocery station. Don't pass by a great bargain there just because you didn't write it down beforehand.

■ Shopping for bread? Consider loaves with thinner slices. These are cheaper, and they make more sense than standard loaves for a lot of people. Dieters, for instance. Or homemakers who make lots of sandwiches for kids. (Ever notice how 60 percent of the sandwich always remains uneaten?)

■ Once a year, check the dates on your canned goods. Throw out any old cans—and, of course, any that are bulging. (This is a bad sign. Food that expands on its own is not doing you any favors. Don't eat it.)

■ Don't buy fast-spoiling fruits like apples, grapes, ripe nectarines, ripe pears, ripe peaches, ripe plums, or watermelons unless you plan on eating them within the next three to five days. For best quality, the U.S. Department of Agriculture doesn't recommend refrigerating these items for longer than that if you can avoid it.

■ The timeline on berries and cherries is even stricter: The USDA recommends using these within two to three days for best quality.

■ If you're thinking of picking up some nice, fresh summer corn in anticipation of next weekend's big cookout, postpone the purchase for a few days. The USDA recommends consuming fresh corn as soon as possible for best quality.

■ Join a local food co-op. (You'll get savings based on bulk purchases.)

■ At the supermarket, check unit pricing closely, even on familiar brands. Manufacturers like to reduce their product sizes by minute amounts but charge the same amount as before. Call me cynical, but I'd say it's a price increase.

■ During the autumn, you can generally expect to find the following types of produce in abundance, at high quality levels, and for a comparatively low price: pears, grapes, zucchini (and plenty of it), sweet potatoes, cucumbers, spinach, chestnuts, and apples.

■ During the spring, you can generally expect to find the following types of produce in abundance, at high quality levels, and for a comparatively low price: onions, new potatoes, spinach, strawberries, peas, artichokes, oranges, and apricots.

■ During the summer, you can generally expect to find the following types of produce in abundance, at high quality levels, and for a comparatively low price: tomatoes, melons, green beans, peas, grapes, peaches, cucumbers, and apples.

■ During the winter, you can generally expect to find the following types of produce in abundance, at high quality levels, and for a comparatively low price: squash, celery, potatoes, cauliflower, cabbage, oranges, onions, and artichokes.

■ Is there a Consumer Supported Agriculture (CSA) farm near you? If so, you may be able to buy organically grown produce at better prices than your local health food store can offer. CSA members (typically city dwellers or suburbanites) pay farmers to deliver the year's harvest as it is collected. It just doesn't get any fresher, and you don't have to worry about nasty chemical pesticides. Ask at your local library about CSA operations in your area. The librarian may be able to point you in the right direction.

■ Some people swear that vitamin supplements are a complete waste of money for everyone except those facing special sets of circumstances (i.e., elderly people, people with diagnosed nutritional disorders, pregnant or nursing women). Ask your doctor if he or she thinks you're spending too much money on vitamin supplements.

■ If you decide to purchase vitamins, you should probably pick a good multivitamin supplement, rather than fifteen separate (and expensive) bottles.

■ Just as an experiment, keep a written record of how much

food you throw away after meals for one week. You'll probably take a whole new approach to food preparation. Keep the list on the refrigerator where you can see it easily!

■ Pizza fiends: For one week, vow not to order pizza or buy frozen pizza. Instead, buy a loaf of fresh French bread, cut it in half, and add your own pizza sauce, mozzarella cheese, and toppings. Bake at 400 degrees for fifteen minutes or so. Like it better? Well, we did. (And there's no one to tip!)

■ Go to church suppers. These are usually $5 to $7 per person, which includes a drink, a dessert, and all-you-can-eat access to the entrée table. The value—and the pleasant company—may make you forget you're making a contribution to a great cause.

■ Put your leftovers in transparent containers. They're harder to ignore, and less food will spoil.

■ Rotate the items in your freezer every time you put away the groceries after a big shop. Bring items you bought last week (or earlier) to the front.

■ Save some energy and some cash. Think twice before you preheat that oven—no matter what the cookbook says! According the U.S. Department of Agriculture, "Recent research has shown that preheating is not necessary, especially for meats and casseroles." The USDA also counsels against preheating the oven when it comes to preparing pies, cakes, and muffins.

■ Don't open that oven door any more than you absolutely have to. Checking every five minutes wastes energy—and money!

■ Don't put a small pan on a big burner. That wastes energy

too. On an electric stove, pick a burner that's appropriate to the pot or pan you're using.

■ Cambridge Books will provide you with a list of food companies that will send you lots and lots of free recipes that happen to use their products. To get a copy of Margaret Smith-White's guide, send a self-addressed, stamped envelope to Cambridge Books, Department A-27, P.O. Box 48382, Phoenix, AZ 85075.

■ Whenever opportunity permits, serve washed vegetables raw. (Sliced carrot sticks, for instance, make a great snack for kids and adults, and they perk up a salad very nicely indeed.) You'll save fuel and nutrients, and you'll probably waste less food, too.

■ You'll use less energy if you plan single-dish meals such as casseroles and stews once a week or so.

■ Shop alone. If you don't have your kids or your spouse sneaking items into the basket—items that are not on your list—you'll meet your goals that much easier.

■ Are there times when you miss berries, sweet corn, and other seasonal foods? Why not freeze them when they come into season. Place berries on a tray in the freezer. Make sure you space them well and keep them at one layer. After they're frozen, toss them into a freezer bag. They'll taste much better then store-bought frozen brands.

■ Specialty shops like bakeries and the local butcher may offer better deals than your local market. Then again, they may not. Check to find out.

■ Have you considered stopping in at bakery thrift shops? This doesn't mean stale bread and donuts. Many companies like Pepperidge Farm, Wonder Bread, and Entenmann's offer some wonderful bargains on cookies, cakes, and, yes, bread. Don't worry, it won't be stale! Check the Yellow Pages to find the ones near you.

■ When shopping at the grocery store, don't select any item while waiting in line at the cash register. If you come across something there you absolutely must have while waiting to check out, get out of line and look for the same item elsewhere in the store. Often you can find the very same brand *cheaper*, in its regular location. I tell you, these marketing people have no scruples.

■ You say the fates have decreed that you have to shop with the kids? Think ahead and bring a bag of popcorn or a piece of penny bubble gum as a reward for good behavior in the store. This may help remove temptation at the checkout aisle.

■ Look below or above eye level at the grocery store. That's where you can often find the best bargains.

■ Check the prices carefully on items on the very bottom shelves. Sometimes clerks don't mark up the prices on every piece. (They don't like bending any more than you do.) Keep an eye out for the relevant items when you hit the checkout aisle; point out the marked cost for the cashier's benefit, and make sure it gets punched in manually.

■ If you're buying prepackaged produce (such as potatoes), weigh it in the produce scale anyway. You're just as likely to find a bag a few ounces under the listed weight as you are to find one that's heavier than marked. Sometimes the packages are up to a pound overweight. For the same price, why not get the one that gives you more for your money? Don't shop when you're hungry. If you pull into the parking lot and suddenly realize you are *really* looking forward to shopping, it may be because you're famished. If this is the case, turn the car back on. Drive over to the gas station and get a can of soda and a candy bar. (I know, I know; I should suggest a bag of fresh grapes and some spring water, but who are we kidding?) The cost of the two will be nothing next to the cost of the mountains of chips and cookies you'd probably buy in the store on an empty stomach.

- Got some extra time on your hands? In the parking lot, sort coupons and go over that list one more time. Do you really need everything you've written down?

- Just as an experiment, during each visit to the market, replace one "convenience" food requiring little or no preparation with the ingredients necessary to make the dish from scratch. It's generally a lot cheaper this way— and the results can be leagues ahead of microwave cuisine. Can you turn the task of preparing the meal into a family or group activity? Your loved ones may find it more rewarding than watching a TV show before dinner. For ideas and recipes, see *The Joy of Cooking* by Irma S. Rombauer and Marion Rombauer Becker or *The Woman's Day Cookbook* by Kathy Farrell-Kingsley and the editors of *Woman's Day*.

- Alternate approach: Buy fewer ready-to-eat items, and consider cooking only one day (or night) a week. Plan all your dinners and lunches for the week ahead, then hit the kitchen. Make lots of casseroles and soups that can be cooked and frozen, then thawed easily.

- Not in the mood to spend a whole day in the kitchen? Then how about cooking two meals at a time? One to eat that night—and another to freeze for later that week. Cooking in bulk leaves you more free time, and chances are you'll waste less by using many of the same ingredients in each dish (half an onion in one dish, the other half in the next dish). Or keep things simple: Just cook twice as much as you need for one night, and freeze half. Stay away from the in-store salad bar. It's no bargain. An apple, a banana, and a cup of yogurt will still be much cheaper than a complete salad at the bar, and you'll be able to manage the quantities to your own preference.

■ Think about changing your office eating habits. Do you stop for coffee and a donut in the morning, then grab a sandwich or the daily special at the cafeteria, followed by a can of soda toward the end of the day? You may just have spent about $10 a day—$2,500 a year—for food you should be paid to even *consider* eating! Buy a reusable, unbreakable coffee mug and bring in your own coffee made from a favorite blend. Bring your lunch and a drink, or keep a refillable water bottle at work.

■ Make your own bread crumbs. It's simple: Take the stale bread you were about to throw away, toast it lightly, and crush it in a food processor or blender. Add some parsley flakes, onion powder, garlic powder, pepper, and whatever else strikes your fancy.

■ Try the same thing with croutons. Cut the bread into cubes, sprinkle them with seasoning, and toast them lightly. Experiment with seasonings: Cajun spices, garlic powder, Parmesan cheese, whatever. Guess what? It's fun, and they taste better than the stuff you get in plastic bags.

■ Did you pick up that newsletter advertising all today's bargains at the front door of your market? An informed shopper will know where the bargains are. It takes only a minute to pull over your cart and check out the deals before you start shopping.

- Joining the ranks of the coupon clippers? File coupons under item and by date of expiration, with the oldest coupons near the front.

- If you've got the time, you may be able to save significantly on your grocery bills by setting aside a little clipping time every week. (Sunday morning, say, after you've finished reading the paper.) Make it a ten-minute-a-week ritual, and you'll see the results in the checkout line.

- Don't clip a coupon for something you never use, no matter how many cents off the manufacturer offers! (If your child is unimpressed with a 50-cent enticement to clean his room, why should you be willing to take the bait?) Be especially wary of those little red machines with the blinking lights that shoot coupons out at you. They are designed to hypnotize you into impulse shopping: "Must buy Everbright Tooth Polish with Bleach Beads. Must buy Everbright Tooth Polish with Bleach Beads." Remember *Invasion of the Body Snatchers*? The people who touch those coupons turn into pod people!

- Plan your trips to the grocery store as if you were planning the Normandy invasion. Lay out a menu for the whole week. Check with ingredients you already have at home, so you won't be buying twice. Make sure you're getting the most out of your food nutritionally. Check your coupon collection (if you have one) and any circulars for items *that appear on your list*. Make sure you have identified at least one modestly priced "fun" food item for purchase. When you're "good to go," hit the streets and head for your prime targets first!

- Someday when you don't actually *need* to go food shopping, go to the store with your typical list in hand. Armed with a calculator and notepad, check to make sure you're not overlooking better values, or new foods that might be easier to prepare or healthier. Add these to your hypothetical list. When you get home, create a new shopping list using the new finds and keeping a few of the old favorites that still represent good values.

■ Consider purchasing the store's house brands. Often these are the very same product as the premium brand and have simply been repackaged. The cost can be much lower. Why? Because the store spends much less on packaging and marketing than the brand-name supplier does. If the store's brand of dishwashing liquid gets your dishes just as clean, and nobody ever sees the label, what's the problem?

■ If you have enough people at home to drink it, always try to buy your milk in half-gallon or 1-gallon containers. You may save 10 to 20 cents per quart by buying the larger size.

■ Nonfat dry milk is a good buy and will store well in a cool, dry place for several months. Try using it, reconstituted, of course, when cooking.

■ Grated cheeses always cost more than cheese bought in wedges and sticks. Think of the forearms you could be building by doing your own grating.

■ Cottage cheese with added fruit always costs more. Couldn't you put the extra stuff in yourself? The fruit, I mean, not chocolate chips or crumbled-up Oreos. (Let's not forget why we're eating cottage cheese in the first place.) Besides, your fresh fruit will taste better than the less-than-fresh variety the store-brought carton will contain.

■ Stay away from name-brand chicken. I don't care how

funny the guy selling the chicken is. The chicken sold under the store's brand name in the plain yellow package cooks up just as appealingly.

■ Get the most out of your more expensive meat and poultry items by using them a second time in leftovers such as casseroles, sandwiches, and salads. Leaving them to shrivel in the refrigerator is such a cruel way to go. See the *U.S. Department of Agriculture's Home and Garden Bulletin no. 183.*

■ Trying to get the most out of an inexpensive cut of meat? Don't forget the marinade. The right one can make a tough cut of meat tender and very flavorful indeed.

■ Stay away from bottled marinades that come from exotic locales such as Maui and Singapore. Instead try the dry-packaged varieties of the same flavors. Same result, better value. Or better yet, avoid pre-packaged foods all together and make your own marinade from a cook book.

■ Another good marinade: salad dressings you already have on hand. Italian, Caesar, and honey dijon varieties can be good on both chicken and meat. This is also a great option if you're cooking for one and wouldn't be able to use an entire package of marinade.

■ Finished shopping? Don't load the stuff into the car just yet. Pull your cart over and go over that sales slip. The scanner doesn't always get everything right. A recent television exposé showed how some supermarket chains have a remarkable tendency to favor the store rather than the shopper. If you spot a mistake, take your receipt to the customer service counter. They can take care of any problems—and you won't be holding up the line by raising a question.

- What do you do with your bottles and other deposit-bearing containers? Do you clean them out, store them, and leave them beside the curb for pickup by your town's recycling program? There's money in every container! Return them yourself and add that money to your savings account. Hey, it adds up, right.

- No one's saying you have to eat at home *all* the time. When you do treat yourself to a dinner out, don't forget the doggie bag. Don't be ashamed; I've seen this done at every chic establishment from the Ritz to the 21 Club!

5

From the Garden

Green is beautiful—and, often, cheap! Part of the reason a garden is a great value is that it's a hobby that gives you something back: produce you don't have to buy elsewhere. Besides providing you with some satisfying homegrown recipe elements, your garden or window box can be a great source of inexpensive gifts for people who *don't* have gardens. ("No, really, thanks, but I already have eighty tomatoes. What? You need me to take two more? Okay, but you have to take twenty of my zucchinis.")

- Head to the library and check out *The Reader's Digest Illustrated Guide to Gardening.* It will help you make the best choices for planting fruits and vegetables in your part of the country.

- Worried about rabbits, raccoons, and other hungry beasties robbing your garden of its treasures? Join the club. But this is a battle you can—and should—choose not to fight. Yes, you can buy fencing, plant it deep in the ground in the hope that the critters won't be able to dig underneath, and attach an extension way up on high in an attempt to keep them from climbing over. Alternately, you cut put up low-voltage, high-expense electric fencing. Either way, it's going to cost a lot of money, and it's *not going to work*. Animals have been getting into people's gardens since the Ice Age. There's nothing you can try to put in their way that they haven't already figured out. So give up, and save yourself some cash. The best real-world solution I ever heard of along these lines came from a friend of mine who suggested that I plant an extra row and simply consider it the animals' commission.

- My advice: Stay away from annuals (plants that only bloom for a single year). Buy perennials. They bloom every year and can often by divided for later garden expansion plans.

- Swap perennials with your neighbors. Divide what you have into good-sized batches, and forget about repotting. Just place everything in a wheelbarrow and head over to their place. Offer to help replant *your* perennials at their place—if you can take some new plants home for yourself.

- Canning? A great way to make additions to your pantry from your garden, and, with a twist of ribbon and a card, an inexpensive, highly personalized gift. Two words to bear in mind, though: *Clostridium botulinum*. Me, I'd avoid that part. Nothing says careless to your friends and family like giving them food poisoning. Yes, it's a gift that keeps on giving, but not the way most of us would prefer. See *The Joy of Cooking* by Irma S. Rombauer and Marion Rombauer Becker for a full rundown on safe canning techniques.

- One piece of eminently sound advice from *The Joy of Cooking* worth passing along here, though—*never, ever "test" home-canned nonacid items by tasting them straight from the jar before they have been cooked*. Cook whatever you have canned in *boiling* liquid for fifteen minutes (the minimum for home-canned vegetables) to twenty minutes (the minimum for home-canned poultry, fish, and meat items). Save yourself a nice expensive trip to the hospital. Boil your stuff as the experts recommend.

- For another source of information about the ins and outs of the canning process, write the U.S. Department of Agriculture, Independence Avenue, Washington, DC 20250. Ask about *The Complete Guide to Home Canning and Evaluating Home Canning Recipes for Safety* (Fact Sheet EHE - 705).

- Before you try to undertake any canning project that involves oils or garlic, talk to an expert. These can be very tricky and may present serious health problems if mismanaged.

- Home-grown herbs provide you with a nearly endless resource for personalized gifts—and for adding wonderful little touches to your own home. But if you're just starting out, buy them already grown as small plants. It's much easier than growing them from seed, and you'll be able to use the plants more readily. (Many a beginning herb gardener has given up in frustration after investing a good deal of time and money in seeds and supplies.)

- Many herbs flower beautifully and grow to be quite large after only a year or two. When they get too big for your garden, pot them in (inexpensive!) terra-cotta planters and turn them into gifts!

- Don't assume that you have to use pesticides in your herb garden! Most herbal pest problems can be solved by spraying a strong jet of water on the plants for three or four days straight, twice a day.

- Water didn't do the trick? Use this cost-effective (and environmentally responsible) insecticide: a mild solution of dish soap and water. Instead of buying the stuff with the skull-and-crossbones warnings, spray your plants (herbs and other plants) lightly with this mixture about once every other day for a week, or until the pests disperse.

■ Another back-to-basics insecticide that will do your pocket-book (and Mother Earth) proud: a box of ladybugs. These are great for killing lots of unwanted pests, and they're much cuter than aerosol cans covered with fine print. Ask about buying a box of bugs at your local greenhouse.

■ Want to find out more about how to stop buying expensive (and environmentally hostile) pesticides for your garden? Contact the Public Information Center of the U.S. Environmental Protection Agency at 401 M Street SW, no. 3404, Washington, DC 20460. Ask for the environmental fact sheet *Home Gardening*, which outlines pesticide-free gardening methods.

■ Save on seeds. Grow houseplants from cuttings you get from friends.

■ Starting a garden? Don't waste time and money planting something that won't grow in your part of the country. Write the Superintendent of Documents at the U.S. Government Printing Office, Washington, DC 20402. Ask for the Plant Hardiness Zone Map. It's only $6.50—and you'll save lots more than that in time and materials when you use it.

■ You say you're a city dweller who's outgrown the old window box? Check out (or start) a local community garden, typically found in a donated vacant lot. Call the owner and make a proposal if you have to. It's great P.R. for his company, and what good is the lot doing the company now?

■ Plant carrots in your garden. They're rich in beta carotene, which a number of clinical tests have shown to prevent cancer. Beta carotene has also been shown to reduce vision loss.

■ We all know that roses can be expensive—but if you buy and plant only one rosebush a year (that's about $12 to $20) you'll save some money *and* add value to your home.

■ Speaking of roses, when their petals are dried and combined with herbs and other flowers (such as lavender), they make great potpourri. Tie everything inside a small cloth pouch. Add essential oils to refresh. Isn't that nicer than buying the latest plug-in room freshener? And it's less likely to short out the building!

■ A further installment in the don't-buy-it-yourself home-study course: Making things with herbs and flowers often involves drying blooms or whole plants. Probably the most effective way to dry herbs is putting them in your oven on the *lowest* setting. Remember, you are drying, not cooking. This may take several hours, but your yield should be quite high. You can also use your microwave. Heat at one-minute intervals at 50 percent power. Turn occasionally. You can purchase herbs already dried, but remember, this will add to your cost!

■ Here's another great reason to hit the dirt on a pleasant weekend afternoon: Well-established gardens increase the value of your home, sometimes quite dramatically. So start digging now!

Herbal Remedies

Your garden may help you take advantage of aromatic and herbal remedies that are much more pleasant (and less expensive) than over-the-counter remedies. (See the items following.) People have used these remedies for hundreds of years; they're believed to have curative effects, and, of course, they smell great. These preparations make great gifts: Cut cheesecloth into 3- or 4-inch squares, or use pretty handkerchiefs (either found at flea markets or made using thin remnant fabric. Fill with dried herbs or flowers and tie with a ribbon. If giving an assortment of scents, tie each sachet with an appropriately colored ribbon. Wrap each packet separately in tissue paper, then place all in gift box or cloth bag. Put together a home-decorated card that details what's thought to be good for what.

■ Lavender and chamomile flower head sachets are said to work wonders for tension and anxiety.

■ Sweet marjoram and orange mint sachets are believed to relieve headaches.

■ Rosemary sachets may help congestion and relieve other cold symptoms.

■ Sage sachet is recommended for relaxing sore muscles.

■ Sleeping pills are iffy from both a financial and, in some cases, a psychological standpoint. Dried roses, lavender, and mint, on the other hand, have been proven to relax and induce sleep. Dry them and sew into sachets or pillows. You'll be amazed how effective these natural sleeping aids are.

■ Flax seed, crushed lavender, and crushed mint sachet, when combined, are also said to help with sleeplessness. (I've tried this myself with very good results.)

■ A dried oat (from your pantry) and rosemary sachet, when combined, are said to help relieve the symptoms of some allergies and respiratory ailments.

■ A variation on the sachet approach: scented pillows. The theory here is a small pillow, placed either on the eyes or against the cheek as you rest, can impart many medicinal effects. (They smell great, which is reason enough for me.) The pillows may be small or large; they large one is basically an adaptation of a standard pillow pattern, with a sleeve inserted in the back for a smaller herb-filled pillow. For fabrics, take a look at remnant bins—or use clean, old, patterned handkerchiefs, either alone or sewn together in a crazy quilt. These mark marvelous gifts and are quite inexpensive.

■ Scented powder. You can make an easy, inexpensive, and striking cosmetic gift—scented powder—by mixing finely crushed dried herbs from your garden with cornstarch and essential oils (experiment with the proportions of each). Place the powder in a box wrapped in pretty paper and include a puff. (You can get one at a beauty supply shop.) Warning: Tell the person to open the box carefully—or expect a messy surprise instead of a gift!

■ Fill a clean old sock with dried whole oats. Tie off securely with a rubber band. Throw the sock in the tub and turn on the warm water; squeeze occasionally. Whoever takes this bath will get a soothing skin treatment appropriate for chicken pox, sunburn, and the like.

■ For a lovely hair rinse for women, simmer rosemary from your garden for about half an hour in spring water. Bottle in plastic spring water bottles (that's the safest way to go in the bathroom, anyway) that have had their labels removed. Use it yourself to add a sweet scent to your hair, or adorn with pretty tags listing ingredients and best wishes.

■ A hair-color rinse that yields an attractive blond shade can be made the same way using chamomile flower heads. Use it yourself or send as a gift—to someone who won't take offense at your suggestion that she color her hair!

6

Vacations and Travel

Why are you going on a vacation in the first place? To relax, remember? And you can't relax if you're going on a vacation you can't afford. There's lots of ways to unwind away from home without spending a fortune. Just think, once you're done, you can come back from your respite, rested and with enough change left in your pockets to be able to sit back, order a pizza, and maybe even rent a video your first night home.

- First of all, plan ahead. Set up a short-term savings plan for your trip. Set a limit to the amount you are willing to spend on the trip. Then add 5 percent more to that amount for a cushion. Do not, under any circumstances, spend more than that amount! (Unless, of course, a loved one has to be bailed out of jail for some reason. And you feel like springing the person.)

- If you're looking for a good hotel, bed-and-breakfast outlet, or other lodging option, why not let the residents of cyberspace to the research work for you? On the Internet, there are bulletin-board groups focusing on local issues for every major metropolitan area in the country (and a good many not-so-major metropolitan areas, for that matter). Post a note specifying your intended destination and the time of your trip, and ask for help in tracking down the best lodging value. You'll probably get multiple responses, and you may even strike up friendships with a few electronic pen pals! Whatever leads you get are absolutely free, and the correspondents on the boards tend to be quite well informed.

■ You can also use the regional-topic Internet bulletin boards to get advice on planning the best driving routes to your destination.

■ Another application of the Usenet regional-topic newsgroups resource: finding the best local shopping values in a particular category.

■ Or use the regional-issue boards to help you resolve whatever uniquely expensive travel-related monkey wrench has suddenly been tossed into your plans. All you have to do is post an electronic note! The information you can get from the boards is limited only by your imagination. Here is a list of the relevant major boards as of this writing; all are easily accessible through the Usenet portion of the Internet. Alas, not all destinations are blessed with a regional-interest board; the list below represents the best information available at press time. (Check with your on-line service provider for advice on the best ways to access the Usenet function and post to these boards, or others that may help you resolve questions.) For Alabama: alabama.general • For Arizona: az.general • For Arizona (Metro Phoenix): phx.general • For California (statewide): alt.california. ca.general • For California (San Francisco Bay Area): ba.general • For the District of Columbia: dc.general • For Florida: fl.general • For Georgia (Metro Atlanta): atl.general • For Illinois (Metro Chicago): chi.general • For Indiana: in.general • For Maryland

(Metro Baltimore): balt.general • For Louisiana: new-orleans.general • For Minnesota: mn.general • For Missouri (Metro Kansas City): kc.general • For Missouri (Metro St. Louis): stl.general • For New England (Massachusetts, New Hampshire, Connecticut, Maine, Rhode Island, Vermont): ne.general • For New York/New Jersey/Connecticut (Tri-state area/Greater New York City area): nyc.general • For Ohio: cle.general • For Oregon: or.general • For Pennsylvania (Metro Pittsburgh): pgh.general • For Pennsylvania (Metro Philadelphia): phl.general • For Tennessee: nashville.general • For Texas (Dallas/Fort Worth): dfw.general • For Washington State: wash.general

■ Another helpful cyberspace approach: Use your World Wide Web browser to access the Yahoo search engine. You'll find it at http/yahoo.com • From there enter the word "lodging" as a search item and scroll through the results until you reach the line for Yahoo's *Business and Economy: Companies: Travel: Lodging* page. On that page, you'll find lots of great leads for tracking down the best bargains when it comes to hotels and accommodations.

■ Have the car checked out completely by a trusted mechanic to make sure it's ready for the wear and tear of a big trip. It will be less expensive to make small repairs at home than big ones at some last-chance garage.

■ Pack your own goodies and lunches in a cooler in the car. They'll be much cheaper (and healthier) than the drive through variety.

■ Don't use the hotel's phone service. Charge your calls when staying at hotels. Check with the manager about phone card protocols before you place any call.

■ Traveling on business? Ask the hotel you're considering staying at about corporate rates.

■ Bringing your pet on a vacation? Make sure he or she has an identification tag that spells out your home address and phone number.

■ Make your hotel reservations well ahead of time, but don't call the national chain's 800 number to do so. It's often cheaper to call the hotel where you plan to stay directly, via its local number. You will often find a cheaper rate that the national center is not promoting or is unaware of.

■ Ask about weekend package deals. If you don't ask, you may be charged the higher amount.

■ Ask whether kids stay free (or at least at a discount).

■ Ask whether kids eat for free (or at least at a discount). This marketing ploy is more common than you might think!

■ When you get to the hotel, ask at the desk if the hotel manager can make you an even better deal. It can't hurt to ask in person, right? Sometimes this results in a reduced rate (especially if you're looking particularly bedraggled from all that road duty).

■ If you are in the military (or reserves), ask if there's a military rate. You'd be surprised how many places have one. Have your ID ready if asked for verification.

■ Is your pet traveling with you? Look for the book *Pets Are Permitted: Hotel, Motel, Kennel and Petsitter Directory*. Not only will it tell you what accommodations will welcome you and your four-legged friend, it will also list appropriate restrictions, room rates, fees, and deposits. Also included: listings for approved kennels for day boarding, a toll-free number to help you locate a local vet if you need one, and campgrounds that will also welcome your pet. Essential reading if you're trying to find the best value in one of these areas. Ask for it at your local bookstore or library, or order by calling this toll-free number: 800-274-7297.

■ Do some investigating into the states you will be passing through and staying in. Are there any national or state parks or historical sites worth checking out? You can reach the National Park Service by calling 800-549-5754.

■ Have your kids keep a journal of your trip. Buy a blank hardcover book. You can find one in any good art supply store or bookstore. Get some tape, too. Ask them to include ticket stubs, photos, postcards, and even pressed flowers. If your kids are too young to write, they can draw a picture of the day's events. And it may just distract them from the greaseburger outlets on the highway, beckoning you to abandon that lunch you packed.

■ If you can't beat 'em, join 'em. Give each child who's old enough to understand the concept a modest travel allowance. Let the child decide where and on what they want to spend their share of the loot. Remind the child often that once the money is spent, it's gone. If someone wants to spend everything on a rubber Indian tomahawk for sale at roadside stand, no problem. But don't back down when the tomahawk doesn't look quite so spiffy a hundred miles down the road. Let the child know that he or she has the option of keeping all or part of the cash to spend when everyone gets back home.

■ For a wealth of good advice on getting the best value for your air travel dollar, call the U.S. Government Printing Office and order a copy of *Fly-Rights: A Consumer Guide to Air Travel*. It's only $1.75, and you'll save far more than that on tickets. To order, call 202-512-1800.

■ Looking for a way to get someone to pay you while you're

on vacation? For a low-cost cross-country trip, hire your-self out to drive someone's car across the country.

- Biking trips can be a lot of fun. Your public library probably has local maps of biking trails that are perfect for weekend excursions. (Bike to a friend's house and stay overnight! Call first, though.)

- How long has it been since you went on a picnic? The fare doesn't have to be fancy if the setting is right. A loaf of bread, a jug of...grape juice, loved one! You're all set.

- Visiting Washington, DC? Call your congressional repre-sentative's office to get free V.I.P. passes to the White House tour. You'll spend less time in line.

- Whenever you can, purchase airplane and train tickets at least two weeks in advance. Also, look for the airfare deals advertised every few months in the newspaper.

- Staying home? Take a self-guided tour of local historic sites. Check your phone directory for the local National Parks Service office; it will be able to provide you with all the information you need.

- If you live near the water, you may be able to take a trip on a sightseeing boat around the harbor for just a few dollars. Don't let the tourists have all the fun.

- For your next vacation, consider trading houses with friends in another part of the country. It takes some scheduling work, but it's worth it. Lodging costs: zero dollars. (You may even find your house in better condition than when you left it, but that depends on your friends.)

- There are two reasons to go to a ski lodge on vacation: to ski and to be seen skiing. If you forget the second reason, you can have a lot more fun and spend a lot less money. Who needs that new Day-Glo parka, anyway?

- Try the smaller, simpler lodges, the ones with fewer amenities such as chic restaurants and fancy ski shops. The rates are usually better. What are you really missing? You can always eat down the road at some more reasonable restaurant. And I don't think you're going to find any great deals on winter clothing at the ski boutiques found in the bigger lodges.

- Timing is everything: Ask if the lodge has any special deals during the season—perhaps a special designed to entice people to visit during a slow time for the lodge.

- If you're feeling adventurous, check into fall skiing. Sometimes it's actually *free!* But wear your oldest skis. The going can get very rough.

- Look into deals on spring skiing, too. You may be able to have all the snow, all the fun, and plenty of sun, so you can pick up a tan, too!

- More often than not, cheap skiing equals poor skiing. But with the right attitude and the right (i.e., old) equipment, you can still have lots of fun.

- Many ski areas have lots of activities going on other than skiing. Look into snowshoeing and guided winter hikes.

- Cross-country skiing is much less expensive than the down-hill variety. Safer, too, for that matter. It's still lots of fun.

- Many of the ski areas make for great hiking in the fall when the leaves are changing. Sometimes you can even catch a free ride up the mountain on the ski lift.

- Many seaside resorts are still open in the winter. Look into a winter trip to the beach. The sea is still beautiful in a completely different way. Call ahead to find out about restaurants and other activities that might still be open and running during the off season.

- Use your World Wide Web browser to access the Yahoo search engine. You'll fine it at http:/yahoo.com • From there, enter the word "lodging" as a search item, and scroll through the results until you reach the line for Yahoo's *Business and Economy: Companies: Travel: Lodging* page. On that page, you'll find lots of great leads for tracking down the best bargains when it comes to hotels and accommodations. You'll also find the entry for *Ski-Gram*, which features the latest bargains in ski lodging. It's updated daily, so give it a look.

- Over the river and through the woods: Vacationing at Grandma and Grandpa's house can be fun. They love you and your kids. They easily forgive small mishaps and may even babysit once in a while. And the fact that accommodations are free on this vacation is certainly a nice bonus. Never come empty-handed, though. Bring some groceries with you (you can stop at the store nearest to Grandma's) and then sit down with your parents and make out a list of some other things you can buy to make your stay less of a financial burden for them. With the money you're saving on the hotel costs, you can certainly afford to help with the groceries.

- If your parents won't hear of you helping to pay for anything, look for some other way to make your stay an advantage for them. See if the gutters need cleaning or anything might need painting. Is there any job around the house that might be hard for them to take on alone?

7

Education

Yours, the kids', your spouse's—whoever's out to learn a little more, that person is making the best possible investment. Here are some ideas on getting the very most from the system, even if you don't have a lot of money to throw at it.

- Do you spend a lot of time watching the local public television station? No wonder; it's usually got the very best stuff on the air. Call or write the station and ask for a list of upcoming programs you can watch for college credit.

- Eager to find an affordable way to put a little extra oomph into your resumé? Look into adult education classes at your local community college.

- Your employer may pay for some or all of the night courses you need to take to become more effective on the job. Ask at your personnel or human resources office for details.

- If you live near a prestigious, nationally known college or university, call and find out whether there's an extension program you can take advantage of. These are usually quite modestly priced. Again, it's a real resumé-booster.

- Before you buy expensive educational software, take a look at Word Rescue software from Titanium Seal. It's entertaining, educational, addictive, and probably the best value in early-reader software available. (It lists for about $5 without registration.) Write Titanium Seal at P.O. Box 291100, Davie, FL 33329.

- Considering a law degree? Write away for a copy of the *Review of Legal Education of the United States: Law School and Bar Admission Requirements*. It's free. You can get a copy by writing the Law School Admission Council/Law School Admission Services at Box 40, 661 Penn Street, Newtown, PA 18940.

- Considering investing in an MBA degree? Before you set your sights on a particular program, take a look at *MBA Q & A*, a thirty-page pamphlet that gives you good advice on career paths, financial aid, and the tests you'll need to prepare for. The booklet is free. You can get it by writing the Graduate Management Admission Council (GMAC), 2400 Broadway, Suite 230, Santa Monica, CA 90404.

- Fax attack! If you need help in a particular research or consumer information area, you've already paid for a specialized report—just by being a red-blooded American taxpayer. What's more, you can get up-to-date fax reports on the status of the information you need. The Superintendent of Documents at the U.S. Government Printing Office now offers twenty-four-hour-a-day fax service. Just call 202-512-1716, then follow the easy voice instructions.

- The American Printing House for the Blind distributes educational materials adapted for students who are legally blind and enrolled in formal educational programs below the college level. If you think someone you know could benefit from the program, write for details. The address is American Printing House for the Blind, 1839 Frankfort Avenue, P.O. Box 6085, Louisville, KY 40206–0085.

■ The Department of Education supports postsecondary education of people who are blind or hearing impaired through its regional postsecondary education centers and single- and multi-state projects serving deaf and blind children and youth. For information, contact the Division of Educational Services, Office of Special Education Programs, U.S. Department of Education, Washington, DC 20202.

■ The HEATH Resource Center is a national clearinghouse for postsecondary education for people with disabilities. It offers information about disability issues, education and training opportunities, and accommodations in the workplace and in post-high-school learning environments. Write for information: HEATH Resource Center, 1 Dupont Circle, Suite 800, Washington, DC 20036. Or call 800-544-3284.

■ The National Library Service for the Blind and Physically Handicapped has established a network of regional libraries throughout the United States for circulating books, magazines, and directories in braille and recorded form. The network also supplies playback equipment! The service is free to eligible individuals. If you think someone you know could benefit from the program, write for details. The address is National Library Service for the Blind and Handicapped 1291 Taylor St. N.W. 202-707-5100 Library of Congress, Washington, DC 20543.

■ The National Technical Institute for the Deaf is a residential facility for postsecondary technical training and education for people who are deaf. Its aim is to broaden career opportunities for the deaf. For more information, write National Technical Institute for the Deaf, 1 Lomb Memorial Drive, Rochester, NY 14623.

■ Best-kept secret in higher education department: the almighty transfer. Community and state colleges typically cost between $25 and $90 per hour of class. Private institutions can cost, quite literally, hundreds of dollars more. Since employers and the rest of society at large are much more interested in where you *finish* school than where you *start*, why pay top dollar for the whole trip? Especially if your child's high school grades were not strong, you or your child can get the very best value by starting out a local community or state college, amassing a plateful of great grades (not too difficult, given the academic standards at many of these institutions), and then transferring for the last year or two to Prestigious U. You'll need to apply to a bunch of Prestigious U's to increase the odds in your favor, of course.

■ Here's a time-tested variation on the above: study (and excel) at an affordable state college, then transfer to a high-powered graduate school for the professional degree and contacts you will need to succeed in your chosen career.

■ College students: A campus job at the student cafeteria can mean not only money but free food, which counts if you're cutting it close budgetwise.

■ Future college students: Can't afford a computer or laser printer of your own? Many campuses make these available to their students.

■ College students: Keep your student I.D. card with you at all times. Local businesses may offer discounts you can take advantage of.

- College students: Take advantage of the student health clinic or infirmary. Get a checkup.

- Ouch! College textbooks cost too much! Check the library; are there copies on reserve you can use instead? If not, bug the professor.

- Ouch! The professor won't put copies of the textbook on reserve for you. (He's the type who changes one paragraph and issues a "revised" version of his own textbook every year. It usually costs $95, and you have to read the new paragraph to pass the final.) Check out *Books in Print*—see if you can find a less outrageously priced softcover edition at a regular bookstore, or order it directly from the publisher. Funny how the student bookstore usually won't carry this version, isn't it?

- Ouch! Unfortunately, you can't find a softcover edition of the textbook you need. Split the cost of the book with a friend or two, preferably someone who shares living accommodations with you. No sense playing more tug-of-war with the book at exam time than is absolutely necessary.

- Considering starting your own home business? For a good start on a self-study program, take a look at *Starting and Managing a Business From Your Home*, available from the U.S. Government Printing office 710 North Capital Washington, DC 20401 202-512-0132 for only $1.75. Its advice can help you avoid making costly blunders during that critical first year of operation.

- For a free copy of the U.S. Department of Education's helpful, informative guide to the college application and financial aid process, call 800-USA-LEARN and ask for a copy of *Preparing Your Child for College*.

- For information about federal financial aid programs for students, write the Federal Student Aid Information Center at P.O. Box 84, Washington, DC 20044. Ask for a copy of *The Student Guide*.

- If you're preparing for your GMAT (Graduate Management Admission Test), you may want to take a look at *The GMAT Bulletin of Information*. It's free. You can get it by writing the Graduate Management Admission Test/Educational Testing Service (ETS), CN 6108, Princeton, NJ 08541-6108.

- If you're thinking of taking the Law School Admission Test (LSAT), you'll probably want to review the free *LSAT Registration and Information Book*. You can get a copy by writing the Law School Admission Council/Law School Admission Services at Box 500-57, Newtown, PA 18940.

- Preparing for a child's college education is often one of the most important long-term financial goals a family faces. Do yourself a favor and pick up a copy of Richard Lewis's excellent book *How to Pay for a College Education (or Any Education) Without Going Broke*. Ask for it at your local bookstore, or call 800-872-5627. In addition, you can write your state's higher education department and ask for details on state aid programs.

- Looking for an educational bargain? Audit courses at an area college or university. There's no cost, you get the same benefit as the regular students—and you're there because you want to be.

- Researching a particular consumer-related topic? Get a copy of the current *Consumer Information Catalog*. It lists dozens of helpful publications on topics ranging from meal planning to economical home design. Most of these publications are available for a nominal charge, and the catalog is free. Ask for a copy; write to the Consumer Information Center, Pueblo, CO 81009.

■ Is your kid looking for a great topic for a social studies report? Mail the White House (1600 Pennsylvania Avenue, Washington, DC 20500) and ask for a copy of the *The White House Photo Tour Booklet*, which will supply forty pages of color photos and lost of cool facts about the First Residence. It is free to you. (your tax dollars at work!)

■ Is there a chance you've got a budding financial wizard on your hands? Write to the National Association of Investment Clubs, 1515 East Eleven Mile Road, Royal Oak, MI 48062, for all the facts on learning about how to start or enter a stock investment club. Talk about a practical skill!

On-Line Learning

If you subscribe to an on-line service that opens onto the Internet, you already have access to the biggest, baddest, most affordable "university" available. Listed below, you'll find a few samples of the incredible (and ever-changing) variety of cyberspace learning options, most of them offered free of charge by educational institutions. Just because you can *learn* for free doesn't mean you get *credit* for free, of course. Contact the university directly, via the e-mail address listed in the home page or other identifying site, if you want information on obtaining credit for your cyberstudies. Obviously, you have to pay for any connect fees through your on-line service provider at whatever rates you've agreed to.

Warning: Exits on the information superhighway open and close with dizzying speed! Fortunately, the entries below will lead you to institutions that are likely to be around for a while, even if the particular courses discussed are changed or phased out. In the case of World Wide Web addresses (the vast majority of what follows), the first portion of the address is likely to lead you to the home page of the educational institution you're trying to reach. If you can't get through by using an address cited below, lop off chunks of it from the right-most section of the address until you reach something that looks helpful. Take what follows as a tantalizing sampler of *some* of the options available, and as an indication of which institutions are taking the most active approach to getting their materials accessible on-line. By the way, none of the course materials that follow can be reproduced for profit. If you aren't familiar with the World Wide Web, ask your service provider for details, or see John R. Levine and Carol Baroudi's excellent book *The Internet for Dummies*.

- Your first stop should probably be the World Lecture Hall, an exhaustive listing of college and University courses that provide World Wide Web home pages of one kind or another. The many disciplines listed and classes supported are enough to impress anyone—but there's a catch. Most of the Web sites indicated are there for the convenience of the paying students, and aren't much use to outsiders. Some of the World Lecture Hall's listings, however (I'd estimate about 15 percent of them) lead to truly fascinating self-study sties and text resources. The World Lecture Hall is definitely worth a look—if you've got the time, and if your service provider has granted you terms that make a leisurely stroll through the ivy-covered walls of Cyberspace U. financially feasible. If you're paying $12 an hour, though, don't bother. You can use the World Lecture Hall by pointing your Web browser to http://www.utexas.edu/world/lecture and selecting from the menu options that appear on your screen.

- Just as mind-numbing in its informational load, and more outsider-friendly, is the World Wide Web Virtual Library.

This is a listing of subject-oriented databases that looks as though it's capable of pointing you toward any and every fact on the face of the earth, though that's probably a bit of an overstatement on my part. Put it this way: It's big. You can use the World Wide Web Virtual Library by pointing your Web browser to http://www.w3.org/hypertext/ DataSource/bySubject/Overview.html and selecting from the menu options that appear on your screen.

■ Or you may want to check out University Online, a massive collection of courses gathered from a broad array of educational institutions. This boasts a very impressive catalog indeed. Downloading special software is necessary before you can use the system, but the payoff certainly seems to be there: University Online offers courses on a staggering variety of topics and at any number of skill levels. Check it out. You can reach University Online by pointing your Web browser to http:// www.uol.com and selecting from the menu options that appear on your screen.

■ For a complete introductory accounting course that includes text, assignments, cases, and tests, check out the site Professor Donald L. Raun of California State University at Northridge has set up. You can get there by pointing your Web browser to http://www.csun. edu/~vcact00g/acct.html/and selecting from the menu options that appear on your screen.

■ A complete course entitled The Holocaust in Historical Context is available on-line through North Dakota's Dickinson State University. You can reach it by pointing your Web browser to http://www.dsu.nokak.edu/course/art-science/socbehav/holocau.html and selecting from the menu options that appear on your screen.

- Chaim Goodman-Strauss offers a course entitled Symmetry and the Shape of Space, an exposition on the connections between symmetry and topology. You can reach it by pointing you Web browser to http://www.geom.umn.edu/~strauss/symmetry-unit and selecting from the menu options that appear on your screen.

- The University of Texas at Austin is among the most comprehensive providers of quality educational materials via the Internet. David Anderson offers the American Literature Survey, which includes interactive sites and on-line texts. Point your Web browser to http://www.en.utexas.edu/~daniel/amlit/amlit.html and select from the menu options that show up on your screen.

- Since this book went to press, scores of on-line courses have been added to the World Wide Web. Call the college or university of your choice and ask what on-line education options they offer.

8

With the Kids

Do you know why God made children so cute? So we don't notice how they have a habit of busting budgets. Every time we head out the door with them, there's something they've just got to have: a hat, a candy bar, a home entertainment center. You resolve yourself to be stern. You plan to say no. But then they look up at you with those eyes that are just a tad too big, smiling and looking at you as if you were the greatest person on the planet. And who wants to disprove *that* theory? Herewith some inventive ideas for finding the best values when it comes to playing with, and taking care of, your kids.

- Trying to teach your children about the value of saving money? Write the National Center for Financial Education, P.O. Box 34070, San Diego, CA 92163, for a catalog of helpful publications that may point them in the right direction.

- When peanut butter and jelly for lunch gets dull, don't hit the fast-food outlets. Try using cookie cutters to cut the sandwiches into fun shapes.

- Never buy those children's paint kits. They're way too expensive, and every color ends up being a variant shade of brown. Instead buy tempera paints at your local teachers' supply store in large sizes. Dole out small amounts for each project in washable containers. Buy just the primary colors. Share the magic you remember when your own parents showed you how to turn blue and yellow into (gasp!) green.

■ Skip the latest battery-powered, market driven toy, guaranteed to amuse your kid for all of fifteen minutes. Start a long-term craft-project box. Stock it with bits of yarn, thread, and extra buttons. Don't forget leftover paper towel rolls and that odd last bit of tinfoil. Keep your tempera paints in the box with an economy-size container of glue. Keep it out of reach of the kids until you're there to oversee any creations.

■ Hot cocoa is a winter must—it's both warming and comforting to all those chilly little (and big) kids who come in from an extended snow-angel session. Its a way to make them feel loved without going to the toy store. (By the way, a good snow-angel session beats a rented video as top-notch wintertime kid entertainment any day.)

■ Always make an extra copy of your kids' portraits and other valued color photos; place the copy in an envelope or anywhere it will be safe and won't be exposed to light. Color photos in picture frames will fade over time. Keep a permanent version of the portrait for the family to look at as a special activity together. Then put the photos back! It beats paying to restore the color in an irreplaceable memento.

■ If you have plenty of extras of particular photos, why not give them to the kids and start a photo album project, complete with written reminiscences of what each picture represents?

- When was the last time you played with sidewalk chalk? Break it out the next time one of your kids complains that there's nothing to do and suggests an expensive remedy for the situation. Demonstrate hopscotch—in person, out on the sidewalk. Your kids will forget all about that battery powered Barbie. For now.

- Skip the multiplex—there's entertainment in your own wilderness. Go on a backyard or local-park safari. Pack up the backpacks with sandwiches and juice. Bring along a plastic jar for bugs (grownups: punch holes in the lid) and a notepad to record your findings. Remember to tell your kids that the wilderness they're exploring is home for the little critters you find. Encourage them to put any and all big game safely back where they found it. Try the same activity in another season. They (and you) will probably be surprised by the changes you record.

- Or: Go camping in your living room, complete with tent, sleeping bags, and fire (if you have a fireplace, that is) for roasting weiners and making s'mores. (That's an adult-supervised activity.) Unplug the TV and tell scary stories. Stay up too late. Giggle.

- Blow homemade soap bubbles. This is especially fun if you have a dog. He'll probably feel it's his duty to catch as many as he can. Make your own stuff by mixing about two tablespoons of glycerine (which can be found at most drug stores) with dish soap and water. (Joy and Dawn work best.)

- Skip the plastic superbubble equipment on sale at the local megamall. Try making your own monster bubbles with a piece of string tied into a loop.

- Before giving away any clothes to charity, ask yourself if any of the items might be good to add to a dress-up box.

This can make for more satisfying play than the latest action figure or dress-up doll.

- Don't rent that Power Rangers movie for your kids. Instead...(drumroll, please) *read* to them. Try the Laura Ingalls Wilder books (beginning with *Little House in the Big Woods*); it's an excellent starting point. Not only does story time with your children encourage them to be readers, it also provides even the slightly older child a little close time with Mom or Dad without the embarrassment of actually having to come out and say that he or she needs it.

- Don't buy your daughter her next piece of jewelry. Make it with her! Mix a little salt, some flour, and some water together; experiment with the quantities until you've got a nice solid dough. (Don't eat it—yuck!) Roll the dough into beads with your kids. Make a hole for yarn with a knitting needle. (Carefully; that's an adult job.) Leave the beads in the sun to dry, or bake them at a very low heat until hard. Paint the beads with tempera paint and string them with yarn.

- Ask your local library for a family museum pass. You'll get free or reduced admission on your next visit.

- Do you have a child who wants to buy or rent the latest high-decibel video game? Teach him or her how to play solitaire. (The official rules are in *Hoyle's Rules of Games*.)

- Build a house of cards instead of watching commercial-jammed kids' television one afternoon. Try it on a thick pile carpet first, then work your way up to the tabletop.

- Exchange old toys for "new" ones—ask fellow parents if they'll set up a swap system with your family.

- For a nice weekend family activity, visit a local apple

orchard or farm. Tours and other activities are usually free; what's more, the produce and other items on sale there are often moderately priced. (But you don't have to buy anything if you don't want.)

■ For free advice on getting your child to turn off the TV and turn on to books, write the U.S. Department of Education's Office of Educational Research and Improvement at 555 New Jersey Avenue NW, Washington, DC 20208. Ask for *Help Your Child Become a Good Reader*.

■ Get free pads of scratch paper from local copy shops. Your kids can color on them to their hearts' content.

■ Go on a Sunday afternoon picnic with the kids instead of visiting the local pay-to-play activity-zone center.

■ If you have a teenager in the house who's looking (or, you have concluded, should be looking) for something productive to do for the summer, write the U.S. Office of Personnel Management, Washington Area Service Center, 1900 E Street NW, Washington, DC 20415, or call 202-606-3283. Ask for information about federal summer jobs in your area. A discreet reduction in weekly spending money may be in order.

■ If you have small children but no family in the vicinity, post a note on the board of the local day care center or school and offer to exchange your children's outgrown clothes with older children's clothes.

■ If your child attends preschool or a weekly play group, look into organizing a clothes swap. Put a bulletin up on the classroom board. Swap item for item.

■ Great kids' card games that beat purchased or rented video game entertainment hands down are War, Slapjack, Crazy Eights, Spit. . . . For instructions see *Hoyle's Rules of Games*.

■ Visit the library with your child one day a week.

■ Do you want to brush up on a foreign language? Those cassette-study courses are pretty expensive, and they usually just gather dust in the closet. Head to the library and check out a book on the language and brush up on some new words by teaching them to your kids (or those of the neighbors). Unveil one or two new words a week, and learn together.

■ Looking for some frugal natural decorations for the house? In the fall, go out with your kids and collect some pretty, brightly colored leaves. You can arrange these into shapes, designs, and even people! Press with a warm iron between two sheets of wax paper. Hang in their windows as natural "stained glass."

■ There are a lot of teach-your-preschooler-to-achieve videos out there. For my part, I've always been a little skeptical of the whole undertaking. Rather than laying down $79.95 and pushing for early results, help your child develop the motor skills that will help when it's time to learn to write by cutting out some leftover cardboard into a fun shape of your child's choice. Use a hole puncher and a piece of yarn with the ends wrapped in tape. Have your child play at lacing or sewing through the holes.

■ Can you start an at-home business—and stop paying for child care altogether? Many such businesses, run out of a laptop computer, allow the entrepreneur (you) to work until the kids get home from school, then start in again when the kids are in bed. For some creative ideas on pulling this off, see Paul and Sarah Edwards's excellent book *Making Money With Your Computer at Home.* Who knows? You could strike it rich.

■ Do you have to work five days a week? Look for a job-sharing program at your workplace. If there isn't one, ask the Human Resources Department about starting one.

■ If both of you must work to make ends meet, consider setting up a time-share child care system with a friend or family member. You do the child care duties on the other person's workdays, and vice versa.

■ Spend less time on the road and more time at home with your kids by changing your work schedule. Time stuck in traffic is time that could be (and probably should be) better spent with your family. If your boss needs convincing, write for *The Work and Family Resource Kit* at Clearinghouse, Women's Bureau, U.S. Department of Labor, 200 Constitution Avenue NW, Washington, DC 20210, or call 800-827-5335. Then make a snappy proposal.

■ Change jobs. You'll find some excellent leads on the kinds of employers you should be targeting in an exhaustive article appearing in the October 1994 edition of *Working Mother* magazine entitled "The 100 Best Companies for Working Women" by Milton Moskowitz and Carol Townsend. Even if the data has changed for a particular firm by the time you track the article down at the library, the article will give you a good idea of the range of benefits offered by the most enlightened firms.

9

Your Health

If you're looking for a way to take sensible preventive action or minimize the costs associated with a problem shared by lots of other people, read on.

■ Instead of attending one of those boring insurance seminars, make a list of your family's main medical events. Who got sick from what? When? Who was operated on and why? Bring the written list to your next checkup and review it with your doctor. He may be able to make recommendations for lifestyle changes or other preventative decisions.

■ Words to the wise: In many countries, rice, vegetables, or breads are the main dish—with the meat used as a flavoring agent or side dish. Some researchers think it's no coincidence that these countries have lower rates of heart disease, cancer, and other serious health problems. Give your diet a friendly shift toward the carbohydrates and veggies—you'll save money, you'll be eating healthier, and you might just prefer the taste!

■ Vegetarians spend less on meat and poultry than the rest of us (i.e., they spend zero dollars), and they just might have the lead track when it comes to avoiding some serious health problems later in life. All those artificial hormones... well, it's just a suggestion.

■ Head Start is a child development program that provides comprehensive educational and social services to children between the ages of three and five. To find out whether your child is eligible to take advantage of Head Start, write the Head Start Bureau, P.O. Box 1182, Washington, DC 20013.

■ If there is a young person in your family with a disability, you need to know all about the state and federal aid available to you. Call the National Information Center for Children and Youth with Disabilities at 800-999-5599.

■ The federal government offers funds supporting the Helen Keller National Center for Deaf-Blind Youth and Adults. To find out if you or a family member qualify for the Center's rehabilitation programs, call 516-944-8900 (voice or TDD).

■ If you have an older person in the home and are eager to find out the best ways to manage the significant medical and caretaking expenses associated with the senior years, call the National Council on Aging at 800-424-9046 and ask for a catalog detailing the information they provide.

■ Before you plunk down serious cash for a stop-smoking program, check out the free plan available from the National Cancer Institute. Write them at Building 31, Room 10A18, 9000 Rockville Pike, Bethesda, MD 20892; ask for *Self-Guided Strategies for Smoking Cessation.*

■ Incentive Department: Once you do stop smoking, you'll be eligible for lower insurance premiums.

■ Are you facing a health-care-related financial crisis?

You're not alone. Call the National Health Information Center at 800-336-4797 (301-565-4167 in Maryland) and ask for referrals that will help you resolve the problems you face.

- Ask you pharmacist about generic prescription drugs.

Diet and Exercise

- Form a walking club with friends. When you exercise it's easier to keep with the program.

- You say you absolutely *must* join a health club of some kind? Check out the YMCA or other local civic gym.

- Find out whether your insurance will cover all or part of the cost of joining a gym. Many will.

- Many health care providers offer complimentary or low-cost diet workshop programs, too.

- Okay. You've got your heart set on one of those expensive workout places with the acres of neon and the people in the spandex outfits hanging out by the juice bar. Your best bet is to play one of these clubs off against another. *Don't commit to anything.* Take advantage of whatever try-it-free-for-thirty-days-and-see-how-you-like-it offers you can track down. Try it for thirty days (or whatever the offer is). Then *leave* and try the same thing with the competing club across the street. Eventually, a salesman will try to get you to cough up a check. Offer to pay a figure that fits within your budget, a number *you* come up with. (Ignore the prices on the brochure.) When the salesperson balks, say you've been considering the offer at the competing location. Leave your phone number. Tell the salesperson to call you when the club can meet your price.

- While you're waiting for the call, look into joining a community-sponsored softball, hockey, or basketball team. No neon, of course, but at least you won't have to worry about whether what you're wearing makes the right fashion statement.

- If none of that appeals to you, consider a *home* aerobics program. There are many aerobics classes to choose from on television. Try the ESPN morning lineup, and tape the show if it's scheduled at an inconvenient time.

- Check out your local pawnshop once a month for great bargains on exercise equipment.

- Considering an elaborate brand-name diet program? There are a lot of scams out there. Before you fork over the cash, see how the program shapes up by reading *Facts About Weight Loss*, which will help you separate the wheat from the chaff. Write the Federal Trade Commission, Sixth St. and Pennsylvania Avenue, NW, Washington, DC 20580.

- Eat less red meat. Substitute other, less expensive items as high-protein replacements. (Tuna, eggs, and rice combined with beans are all good candidates—and easier on your arteries.)

- Take swimming lessons at the Y.

- You don't have to pay anyone to help you lose weight. Write for *An FDA Guide to Dieting*, Food and Drug Administration, Division of Consumer Affairs, HFE-88, 5600 Fishers Lane, Rockville, MD 20857.

- If sodium is not a problem for you, and the doctor agrees that it's okay, baking soda, or sodium bicarbonate, could be just what you need for an antacid. Used to be quite popular, you know. Add 1 teaspoon of soda to 6 ounces of water and sip slowly. Baking soda is the only active ingredient in most store-bought preparations. Why pay 30 percent more for a mint flavor?

- Women: Take stock of all your makeup! Yes, even that glittery eye shadow you bought in 1979. Throw out everything you don't wear. Just be brave and do it. Toss any fuchsia blush and blue eye shadow. Smell your lipstick. If it has a slight odor, you know it's a little musty. Toss it. That's mildew. If your mascara is more than three to five months old, toss it, no matter what it smells like. Bacteria can build up and lead to eye infections. Yuck. Nobody needs an extra trip to the doctor and an expensive prescription, right?

10

Frugal Luxuries

A contradiction in terms? Nope. There are plenty of ways to spoil yourself that cost little or nothing—or represent a truly outstanding value. Here are some you shouldn't overlook.

- The zero-dollar, one-night vacation: Don't do any work. Don't stay up and watch TV. Instead, dab a drop of perfume or scented oil on the light bulb. It will fill the entire room with a lovely aroma. Put on a favorite relaxing record and close your eyes. Put your feet up. Do nothing.

- Shopping for silverware? According to the National Retail Federation, January is the best month to buy.

- Looking for the right time of year to indulge your sweet tooth? According to the National Retail Federation, February (after Valentine's day) is the best month to buy candy.

- Instead of punching up a pay-per-view movie, read a book you've been dying to get to.

- Are you prepared to sell an "investment" or "collectible" piece at the right price if an offer is made? No? If you can't bear to part with it, it's not really an investment, is it?

Don't use "investment purchase" as a handy rationalization for picking up stuff you don't need.

■ Become a connoisseur of flea markets and yard sales.

■ Before buying anything from an antique store or flea market, ask if the seller can do any better on the price. By asking this simple question, you may be able to knock 15 to 20 percent off the list price.

■ According to the National Retail Federation, May and December are the months when you can expect to get the best deal on furniture.

■ Give any piece of antique furniture you're considering buying a good jiggle. Careful—only about as hard as it would take to make a pinball machine tilt. Does it feel sturdy?

■ When buying antique furniture, make sure all parts of the furniture are original to the piece. Look for mismatched wood or missing veneer. Are there odd nails that don't match the nails in the rest of the piece? Is any hardware missing—hinges, drawer pulls, keyhole fittings? Do the locks work? Don't pay top dollar for an "antique" that's not antique at all.

■ Is the antique you're considering buying something you're planning to use in your home? If so, can you do so safely and without damaging the piece? Is there a special place in your home for it?

■ Many antique shops will automatically mark down an item's price after a certain number of days. If the purchase isn't of life-or-death importance (and let's face it, it probably isn't), check back in a few weeks to take another look at that price tag.

■ Some pieces of antique furniture may not cost any more

than contemporary ones, but may boast far superior workmanship.

- Next time you want to see a movie, cuddle on the couch and watch the best discount rental you can find at your video store. Our family has snagged some surprising winners this way. Believe it—the cut rate often doesn't reflect the quality of the picture.

- Best winter boot value? It's got to be L.L. Bean. This is one instance where outfits that offer less-expensive merchandise are definitely providing you with false savings. The folks at Bean may charge a little more, but the boots really do last forever, or darn close to it. This manufacturer will resole even ancient Bean boots—and for prices so reasonable, you'll wonder if there's been an accounting error. Spend the up-front money once, and you won't be needing another pair of boots for quite a while. Call L.L. Bean toll-free at 800-221-4221, or write them: L.L. Bean, Freeport, ME 04033.

- If you subscribe to a daily paper but rarely read it, cancel your subscription or limit it to Sundays only. When you really need to catch up on a late-breaking news event, you can go get the paper yourself.

- Collectible books signed by the author are, as a general rule, worth more. The more personalized the inscription, the greater the value.

- Collecting old or rare books? It is often best to collect a single topic, such as American westerns, vintage science fiction, or Victorian children's books. When you have a large enough assortment (about 250 books), the collection as a whole may be worth more than the sum of its parts.

- Don't waste your time or money "collecting" modern

hardcover books by megastar authors in the hope that the volumes will someday be worth something. The initial print run on a Stephen King or Danielle Steel novel may run into the hundreds of thousands of copies.

- Older and/or rare books are great fun to collect and are far more likely to increase in value. Remember that the condition of the book, not merely its status as a first (or early) edition, directly affects the value of the book. Are the pages damaged? Is the binding broken? Is the cover faded? Is the dust jacket missing? All these factors can have a dramatic impact on the book's value. Before you lay down significant cash for a promising older or rare book, check with an independent source for an estimate of the book's value.

- Scan the television listings a week ahead of time for programs you really want to watch or tape. You'll spend less on video rentals. (Use a high-quality videotape for repeated taping.)

- Some collectibles, such as Christmas ornaments, figurines, postage stamps, and jewelry, are always going to be collected. There is less risk in these items. If you're starting to collect something (preferably for both love and money), an area like this is a better place to start than the "limited-edition" Wizard of Oz plates.

- Split a dessert when you eat out.

- Volunteer as a ticket usher at a local community theater. You'll get to see the show for free! Wear comfy shoes.

- If you volunteer for stage crew work at a local community theater, you'll see the show, make some great friends, and get invited to the cast party without spending a dime.

- See if your video store rewards frequent rentals with one for free. If not, suggest it to the management; you never know until you try.

- Forget the fancy hors d'oeuvres you were planning for the next rental-movie night. Instead, make popcorn in interesting flavors, like Parmesan and Cajun spice. The spices are available at your local grocery store for next to nothing, as is (gasp!) popcorn you don't make in a microwave!

- Want to look chic, stay sober, and save a couple of bucks at the next cash-bar party? Order club soda on the rocks with a twist. Sip slowly.

- It's amazing what we'll pay just so we can say we've tried something with a funny name. Have you ever had a really *good* specialty drink at a Chinese restaurant (e.g., a Suffering Bastard)? Me neither. Skip 'em. They cost way too much for the pleasure of drinking something with an embarrassing name out of a Tiki glass. If you have to spend the money on something, stick to what you know.

- The next time you're scheduling a social engagement, consider going out to lunch with someone rather than meeting for dinner. You'll save up to 50 percent on the tab.

- Shopping for a stereo, television, or VCR? According to the National Retail Federation, February, May, and December are the best months to buy.

- If you're planning to hook a VCR up to a small-screen TV, you'll be wasting your money if you pay for the snazzy, high-resolution, heads-imported-from-Denmark model. Low-end VCRs are fine for low-end TVs; the only quality problems you're likely to notice will come when you try to hook up a low-end player to a high-end receiver.

- Is there a discount, second-run movie house in your area?

Often they have excellent foreign films, independent films, and animation works.

■ There's a brisk business these days in new, snazzy looking leather-bound "limited-edition" books by top contemporary authors. Many of the outfits selling them strongly imply that you should consider these volumes financial investments of some kind. Don't. If you decide to buy them, do so because you feel you want to pay $60 for a leather-bound edition of a current bestseller, not because you think the value is going to increase within the next year or two.

■ Whatever is hot as a collectible right now is probably at its highest price right now too. If you are lucky enough to happen across something currently chic at a very good price, ask lots of questions before you put your money on the table. Take a good look at the item. Is it damaged in some less-than-obvious way? Is it really as old as it appears to be? Or are you looking at a bootlegged Partridge Family lunchbox?

■ You can find some fascinating old magazines that make for marvelous (and inexpensive) bathroom reading material. Keep an eye out for them at flea markets and used-book stores.

■ Your library may hold an annual book sale. You can pick up great books for pocket change—and help raise funds for an important local institution.

11

Looking Good for Less

Cosmetics

Hamlet wasn't crazy about it, the animal-rights people aren't crazy about it, and a lot of *guys* aren't crazy about it. But sometimes, for some people, it's just the thing. Here are some ideas for getting the most value for your cosmetic dollar.

■ First issue to consider: Cosmetics are expensive and generally overused. Remember that too much makeup is always too much—and too little is almost always just fine.

■ Feel naked without any makeup at all? Then cut back to the most important elements for your skin tone. For blondes: mascara. For brunettes: blush. For women of color: lipstick. For redheads: a light blush and mascara (especially if your skin tone is pale.)

■ Petroleum jelly makes a good mascara. Use an old mascara brush that has been washed clean to apply it. It's cheap, easy on your lashes, and not animal tested.

■ Petroleum jelly will also remove eye makeup and lipstick.

- Another inexpensive option: Mineral oil is the only active ingredient in most eye makeup removers. Only the fragrance is missing. Keep a bottle on hand and use it instead.

- Milk of magnesia has many of the active ingredients that can be found in expensive facial masks. With a cotton ball, dab on face, let dry, and rinse well with cold water. Your skin will be baby soft.

- Hydrogen peroxide makes a very effective astringent. It's strong, so use it only every other night or so and apply it to a damp face to allow its cleaning action to really kick in.

- Hemorrhoid cream can be used under eyes to diminish puffiness and small lines. Really! (Keep it out of your eyes, though.)

- Generic-Is-Beautiful Department: Remember that most inexpensive cosmetic products often contain the very same active ingredients as the name brands—only with fewer moisturizers or less perfume.

- You can't trademark a fragrance. That's good news for you: Those inexpensive imitations of the name-brand perfumes are pretty much indistinguishable from the real thing.

- Want to treat yourself to a homemade facial? Try steaming your face over a pot filled with very warm water. Cover head and pot with towel. You might even add peppermint or lavender to the water. Be careful carrying around scalding water or inhaling it; if the water feels at all uncomfortable to inhale, then wait and let it cool a little. Then breathe it all in. Aaaahh.

- The final touch? Milk. It's a very mild astringent that will helpremove dead skin cells. Dab it on your face with a cotton ball. Let dry. Rinse. This will leave your skin baby soft.

- Stay away from expensive moisturizing bath bars. Most moisturizers found in soap are rinsed off in the bath. The rest is rubbed off when you towel. Stick with the plain-Jane, 99 and 44/100 percent pure stuff. And try just a drop or two of baby oil in your bath water.

- To make the most out of a moisturizing lotion, apply while skin is still damp from the bath. Let your skin air dry.

Fantastic Hair

Tending to your tresses? Here are some tips for doing so without toppling the treasury.

- Grey hair is beautiful. Don't dye it.

- If you must dramatically change your hair color, then get a professional to do the job. You'll save money, because repair jobs in this area tend to be quite expensive. And just living with that aggressive green tint for the next six weeks probably isn't going to be an option.

- No kidding: Beer (especially *cheap* beer) makes a great hair rinse. It cleans away conditioner buildup and makes for a fun shower—*if* you're old enough. Rinse well afterward with cold water.

- Want to take a crack at cutting your own hair or giving yourself a trim? Hit the library; look through magazines like *Allure* and *Seventeen* for great tips on what to take on yourself. (This is a perennial topic in these publications.)

- If you're making an appointment at a salon, see if the wash and blow-dry are included in the price of the cut. If not, arrive with clean hair and simply have your hairdresser spritz it until it is wet. After he cuts it, opt for the free air-dry rather than a blow-dry.

- Look for salons that offer coupons or special deals for referring customers.

- Check the newspaper for salon specials.

- Beauty supply stores are a good place to look for deals. Ask if the person behind the desk is a licensed cosmetologist. Then ask lots of questions. This person can be invaluable in helping you find the right shampoo or styling brush.

- Never perm your hair yourself or undertake the job with a well-intentioned friend. The damage done will almost always cost more to repair than the cost of a good professional perm.

- Tipping in a salon is the same as in a restaurant, 15 percent or so. Don't feel guilty about tipping in this range. If you really don't like the results, say so and *don't leave a tip*. Then find another salon.

- If, on the other hand, you've got your heart set on visiting a stylist who'll remember your name and recall what looked good on you last time (and what didn't), then head for the small salon with the best rates you can find. Ask whether the stylist keeps a card on each of their customers detailing what worked on previous visits, what you like and don't like done to your hair, and what chemicals were last used. At such a salon, you're more likely to get an honest answer to the question "Will this look good on me?"—and you won't have to spend your hard-earned dough repairing any hatchet jobs.

That Great Outfit

Most fashion consultants cost a bundle, one way or another. Not me! Here's some advice for assembling a fabulous wardrobe on the cheap.

■ We all need at least one great outfit. When you're on a budget, though, the outfit should be versatile as well as affordable. The key to this—for both men and women—is to stick to the classics.

■ If at all possible, avoid buying clothing for occasions that are imminent. We tend to overpay, and to make poorer fashion choices, when we're buying something, *anything*, for an upcoming event.

■ See a clothing item that looks like it would be perfect for your wardrobe—but not your pocketbook? Ask when it will go on sale...and offer to put a deposit down to hold the item until then.

■ Think twice before you buy that fucshia frock. There are only a few colors for women that will work in pretty much any setting. Stick to a "safe" color you can wear on many occasions.

■ The little black dress is indeed the best bang-for-your-buck fashion invention on record. Just don't make it *too* little. You may have to appear in court someday.

■ You say basic black doesn't work for you? You can still find a single, stunning all-purpose dress that won't cost too much. You may well do quite nicely dressed in white. If you feel uncomfortable in this color, try ecru or ivory.

■ Navy is another great option for that all-purpose, won't-cost-an-arm-and-a-leg dress. It can be formal if dressed up with a single strand of pearls (faux or real). It's great in summer with lots of white accessories, and if you add a yellow scarf or a vivid red purse, you'll be ready for a formal event.

Tips for Men

- Men are lucky, in that they don't need as many suits as women do in the workplace, but unlucky in that when they *do* have to wear a suit, a cheap one stands out ever so much more dramatically. I am going to take a calculated risk here and advise men to spend your money on one or two great suits. Stick to the classic and very traditional looking. Don't chase the fads.

- Buy two pairs of pants with every suit. (Pants rip and otherwise self-destruct before jackets do.) Your suit will last twice as long, but you won't *pay* twice as much.

- Take care of your suit. Have it professionally cleaned on a regular basis. It will last longer that way.

- *Do not wear any part of the suit on an informal or nonbusiness occasion!* You spent the money; don't waste it on an impromptu game of touch football.

- The dark navy blue suit is the easiest and the most versatile.

- There are only two colors of dress shirts for a man to wear without taking a risk: white and pale blue. Don't get talked into buying any other colors.

- About ties: Never, ever spend your hard-earned cash on anything that looks even vaguely like a biology experiment. Yes, that includes paisley.

- Ronald Reagan brought back the brown suit. Then he left for California, and you know what? *He took the suits with him.* If you're only going to buy one, make sure it isn't brown.

- Best workplace clothing value of all: Ask your boss to institute a "casual day"—or allow a judicious dressed-down look every working day. One less day to worry about finding clothing of the exact same color, right? Try wearing crisp white or blue button-down with khaki pants in beige, gray, or even an olive tone.

- When renting a tux, don't rent the shoes unless you really have to. They are just way too shiny, and your own regular black dress shoes will probably do just fine.

- Consider buying a used tux if you find yourself renting more than twice a year. These can be had in good condition for $50 or less.

Shoes

Here are some tips on the fine art of securing footwear without applying for a second mortgage.

- When in doubt, buy black. Black shoes go with almost everything and can be resoled easily.

- Buy shoes before noon. (Later in the day, your feet swell somewhat, and this can cause you to buy shoes that are slightly too large, leaving you with blisters.)

- Men: Are you thinking about buying brown dress shoes? Go directly to Jail. Do not pass Go, do not collect $200. You bought a brown suit at some point in your life, and you must now pay the price. All right, all right, I'll bail you out this once. Look for a very dark brown shade. Dark brown shoes will go nicely with most suits.

- Women: Buy only comfortable shoes. You'll be much more likely to wear them, unlike those painful pairs sitting in the back of your closet.

- Women: Keep an eye out for two-for-one deals at the shoe store—but stay within your color needs when you visit.

- Women: Don't become emotional about shoes. Beware the Imelda Syndrome! If you feel a charging fit coming on, leave the store and count to one hundred while breathing deeply. I know, I know, it's easier said than done. Why is this?

- Take care of your good shoes by waterproofing and conditioning them. Stay away from the spray preparations that put more waterproofing into the air than onto your shoes. Stick with a good old-fashioned tin of saddle soap.

- In the summer, but *two* pairs of the cheapest (comfortable) white sneakers. Look for them at the dime store or at the larger discount houses; you can usually get a pair for about $6. I like to wear mine on alternate days.

- These cheap sneakers come in kids' sizes, too. The same two-pair rule applies here, as well. Make the shoes a little more funky by dyeing the shoelaces fun colors.

- Or you can use ribbons, lace, or rickrack as shoelaces. Just make sure they can be tied securely for safety.

- For kids, buy only all-white socks in the largest bag you can find. They're cheap, and you won't have to worry about finding a matching pair for weeks. If you're lucky.

Jewelry

It glitters, it glistens, it enchants—but is it real? Didn't your mother ever teach you that it's rude to ask personal questions?

- Wear only a piece or two of simple jewelry at any given time. Simple gold-tone studs worn alone will look more like real gold than if combined with several *other* pieces of gold-tone jewelry. One strand of faux pearls with a simple clasp is more likely to pass for the real thing if the effect isn't cluttered by other pieces.

■ Wearing cubic zirconium earrings? Your secret's safe with me. This is one case where less is definitely more. If you wear a smaller size, you'll be more likely to get away with it. Are people going to think that you're really likely to own gum drop-sized diamonds? Or wear them to the supermarket?

■ Looking for a fun piece of real jewelry? Antique stores *may* be able to point you toward some great bargains. Before you buy, though, ask the shopkeeper to identify the stone and give you its thumbnail history. Ask if you can have the piece appraised, and return the piece if the appraisal doesn't hold up.

■ Another good place to look for a great deal on jewelry is a local artist's studio or craft fair. Many new jewelers start out selling their wares at these places at rock-bottom rates. They're usually more than willing to bargain, too.

■ Your best bet, for value, is to stay away from precious stones altogether and look into the semiprecious variety. There are many beautiful tones and colors to choose from.

■ Twenty-four-karat gold is wonderful stuff, but it's not the best choice for rings or clasps. This variety of gold is just too soft to withstand the inevitable wear and tear. Four-teen-karat gold is much tougher; it contains other metals (like nickel) that make it stronger.

■ Considering a piece of gold jewelry that is less than 14 karat? Fine—just don't pay a lot for it. There isn't much gold in there. When in doubt, have it appraised.

■ Vermiel gold is really silver that has been plated with gold.

Don't let the jeweler base the cost on the weight of a pure-gold piece.

- Sterling silver is the best silver for content and strength. Many other silvers will bend and finally break. Worth keeping in mind if you're dealing with clasps and fastenings that will get a lot of wear.

- Yuck! Copper can turn your skin green. Instead of heading to the jeweler for a solution, fix it yourself. Try coating the part of the jewelry that touches your skin with a few coats of clear nail polish.

12

Special Occasions

I love living in modern times. Don't you? Not only have the holidays lost most of their original meaning, but they've basically become a competition for who can buy the most stuff, cook the best, wrap the prettiest, and decorate the house in a style most reminiscent of "Busby Berkeley meets Rudolph." I don't think the Pilgrims were up on the roofs of their houses, tacking up light-up candy canes. No. They just cooked a mean mess of maize, and we admired them for all that.

It is possible nowadays to have a beautiful holiday, remember the basic ideas we're celebrating, give thoughtful gifts, and still have money for food at the end of the month. Just follow some of these ideas, and use the others as inspiration for your own inventive approaches. (By the way, for ideas on gift giving for all seasons, see Chapter 13.)

Hanukkah

■ For some great ideas on gift giving during the Festival of Lights, and a review of the underlying themes of this important holiday, see Chaim Rapahael's fine book *Hanuk-*

kah Festival Days: A History of Jewish Celebrations. You can find it at your local library.

■ You may also want to take a look at Leo Trepp's *The Complete Book of Jewish Observance,* which will provide some important details on the traditions associated with Hanukkah.

Christmas

■ Christmas used to be a time of *edible gifts only.* Trees were hung with treats and stripped bare on the big day. If you're facing a tight-budget holiday, you may want to try reinstituting this classic approach. Make the most of a single gift per family member, placing each gift beneath the tree. Open the gifts first, then move on to the main activity—attacking the tree. Don't chomp on pine needles or electric lights, though.

■ Write your Christmas list in October. You will plan your purchases better.

■ Part of a big family? Try a "theme gift" approach: All the adults are assigned one family member and must buy a single gift from one economically manageable category (like CDs or books). It's fascinating to see what turns up under the tree, and it actually makes shopping a lot simpler and more fun. The presents tend to mean a lot more when there are a few very special treats.

■ Some families send the *same* holiday card back and forth each year, adding personalized messages with each exchange. It's kind of like an annual game of holiday tag.

■ Try limiting each family member, including children, to one major gift and one stocking filled with goodies. This approach means less burnout, less chaos, less wrapping paper, and more fun if you target the present correctly. One approach: Make the giver compose (or dictate) a favorite story about the recipient, to be read immediately before the present is opened.

■ Is there a serviceman or servicewoman in your family stationed overseas? He or she may be able to take advantage of a long-standing tradition that's particularly popular at holiday time. A ham radio network known as the Mars Station relays messages all over the world at no charge to pass along messages to loved ones. The final message comes via a phone call from the network operator closest to your hometown. A nice touch—and it beats trying to make a person-to-person call to Korea.

■ Skip this year's big-budget Hollywood smasheroo movie; instead, stay home with the family and read Charles Dickens's *Christmas Carol* aloud.

■ For younger kids, try reading *The Best Christmas Pageant Ever*, by Barbara Robinson. It's available at your local library.

■ Tape *It's a Wonderful Life* so that you don't have to rent it next year.

■ Origami Christmas ornaments made from white paper or from recycled gift wrap are a stunning addition to the holiday. They're easier to make than you think; check your library for books on the subject.

■ Economical Christmas gift update: Personalized cookies and other baked foods will remain fresher during mailing if you place in a zip-lock bag with a single slice of bread. The bread releases its moisture into the baked goods. And you won't get the groans that accompany the gift of a 12-pound fruit cake.

- Don't apologize for homemade Christmas gifts. Revel in them. It's always a nice touch to include a card with the recipe for your gift; sign the card and date it. Your recipe may just become a keepsake.

- Is there an old cookbook or collection of recipes that your grandmother (or other relative) treasured in years past? Use it to put together an old-fashioned treat that may mean much more to the faraway members of your family than any store-bought item. You may just rediscover a Christmas treasure from the Old World—or even an original recipe scrawled in the margins somewhere. If there's a story or tradition behind what you make, all the better. Include the details on a card with your gift.

- The traditional holiday feast can be a huge expense. If you don't have a large family, how about inviting your friends and loved ones to gather and help share in the preparation (and cost) of the big meal?

- Plan ahead if you know that baking is going to be a good portion of your gift giving this year. Buy baking materials in larger, economy sizes. But be careful not to go overboard on this—it's a pain to store flour, sugar, and butter you won't be needing. Grab a calculator and put together a realistic estimate of what you'll need, then take advantage of savings where you can.

- Of course, even unused baking materials don't need to go to waste. See if a shelter or church near you can use any of it before or after Christmas Day.

- When it comes to wrapping Christmas presents, simpler is not only better, it's sometimes a lot more beautiful. In our household, we like the effect of wrapping all the presents in simple brown paper (grocery bags, turned inside out) and fastened with twine. This is a rustic, appealing look that puts the emphasis where it belongs: on that fabulous tree of yours. Who needs wrapping paper?

■ If you feel like jazzing up your Christmas presents, but still aren't crazy about spending lots of money on the shiny store-bought stuff, use gold stickers or layered tissue paper.

■ Looking for a distinctive homemade wrapping paper with the personal touch? Try white paper, with poster-paint hand prints applied from each member of the family.

■ Another intriguing low-cost wrapping variation: sponge-paint designs on newspaper.

■ Yet another great homemade wrapping material is blank newsprint, which can be decorated in any number of ways. You can get it for free by heading out to the printing facility that produces your local newspaper. Ask for the ends of the rolls; they're long, but not long enough to work on the presses. (Don't bother asking at the front desk; head for the back of the facility and ask one of the ink-covered employees if you can talk to the foreman.)

■ Small brown lunch bags make great gift bags for any holiday celebration. For a child's gift, the child giving the gift can decorate the bag using stickers and markers. An adult could decorate it with appropriate cutout phrases and magazine photos. Carefully glue the pieces into place and brush over the whole bag with a light glaze of decoupage. (A clear drying glue, ask for it in a craft store.)

■ If you must buy holiday gift wrap, do so on December 26.

■ Save your Christmas cards; next year, you can clip them into folded homemade gift tags. They don't cost a cent, and they look a lot better than the store-bought variety.

- Empty bank accounts looming as the Christmas season approaches? Yikes. Check out the local mall or department store; ask if they're looking for extra help during the holidays. Their hours are often more flexible during this time of year, and some may actually pay above their normal wage rate during the rush. Many stores are open for longer hours. Sometimes they even ask some of their more enthusiastic holiday employees to stay on full-time. (You'll probably be eligible for an employee discount, which you should use *judiciously*.)

- Or: Find out if a church, community center, or rest home in your town is having a craft fair. Try your hand at selling some of your handiwork. Ask if you can sell baked goods. (The fair itself may hold a concession on the lucrative food table.)

- Or: Post an ad as a cleaning service; offer a special holiday price. Lots of people want to have their homes cleaned who might at other times do the job themselves. But with the holidays being a very hectic season, cleanup might (for the right price) be a service worth paying you to do. Do it yourself, or enlist the help of a partner. Check out the average price of the cleaning services in your area; better their price by 5 percent or more. But keep in mind your time is worth something—and housework is hard work. Don't underpay yourself.

Easter

- Looking for an alternative to the sugar-overload syndrome at Easter time? Instead of lots of expensive, fit-inducing candy in a plastic basket, try one nice (small) stuffed animal and a *few* pieces of candy, all placed in a good-quality basket that can be reused each year. The excitement will build each time the bunny basket comes down.

Halloween

- Forget the cheesy plastic pumpkin or the easy-to-destroy paper bags. Let your kid play the "fill-it-up" game with a big pillowcase. (Theirs, not yours.) It doesn't cost a thing, it lasts longer, it holds more candy, it's reusable (even as a pillowcase), and it may instill greater generosity on the part of the candy benefactor. There *is* all that space to fill up, after all. Make sure Mom and Dad get a cut of the loot for coming up with this idea. (Don't want the little ones to get sugar-blitzed, after-all!)

- Talk your kid out of dressing in "this year's costume." Who wants to be one of eight thousand Power Rangers? Customized, personalized outfits are cheaper, more fun, and may just result in a bigger haul. Make sure your child can see clearly through whatever headgear you develop, and don't forget that the costume should feature some element visible to oncoming traffic.

13

Presents, Any Day of the Year

The pressure, the pressure! Relax. It only *seems* as if some people are impossible to buy for. Here are some ideas you can adapt to virtually any gift-giving occasion.

Holiday Giving

- You say the letter carrier or doorman always gets an (expensive) bottle of Scotch from all the other neighbors, and you've already got some doubts about his capacity for quality control with all that "cheer"? Pick up a nice, affordable scarf; that will warm his or her spirits, too.

- Scarves make great "Secret Santa" workplace gifts, too.

- About that relative. You know the one I mean. The one you see only during the holidays. The one whose interests and passions are completely beyond you. The one who smiles hopefully and gives you an assortment of imported cheese every year. Let's face it: This person feels obligated to give you a gift of some kind, and as a result, you feel the same obligation. Why not call that relative well ahead of time this year and see if you can't work out a new tradition? Ask about trading calendars, coffee mugs, or cologne. Or maybe some Triscuits, for the six years' worth of cheese you haven't eaten yet.

- Buying for a friend or loved one who happens to be a teacher? Forget about that sweater with the image of the yak on it; these people are more often than not scouring their own homes for supplies. What with today's cutbacks and microscopic budgets, a gift certificate from a local teachers' supply store can be used on extra items that would otherwise have to come out the teacher's pocket. Trust me, even a certificate for five dollars helps.

- Another idea for the teacher(s) on your list: Contact the teacher's aide (usually another mom or dad) and enlist their help in organizing a class gift from all the students.

- Tips to moms and dads: I don't know a single teacher who doesn't appreciate home-baked goodies during the holiday season (or as part of a birthday celebration, for that matter). A pleasant, personalized, and inexpensive gift— and if you play your cards right, you'll have all the teachers fighting over who gets your kid next year.

- Write a letter to the camp extolling a favorite counselor's virtues. You just might guarantee the person a job for next summer, which counts for a lot more than that hefty tip you wish you could give. Then write a nice handwritten note to the counselor.

- When in doubt, personalize the gift. Give that trusted friend a little something that represents one of the things you admire about her the most. If she's a great cook, how about a homemade apron in printed fabric?

■ If a friend loves gardening, offer a plant that can be transferred to her outside garden.

■ If someone you know is always carting the kids back and forth from hockey games to ballet classes, how about picking up a relaxation tape or a book on tape for her to listen to in the car?

■ Instead of an expensive print or painting, why not scour the flea markets or garage sales in your area for a distinctive frame? You're much more likely to get a good price on the latter—and you won't have as much trouble picking one that's just right for the intended recipient.

■ Your local health food store can be a great source for materials you can use to make scented ink, a nostalgic (and thrifty!) gift that will be a real treat to friends who love to write letters. Combined with a box of off-price stationery and a calligraphy pen, the ink can make an extremely thoughtful under-$10 gift. Buy the ink in a bottle. Remove the label by soaking the bottle in warm water. Then make your own label, decorated with drawings of flowers. (If you're not feeling artistic, use flower stickers.) Using an eyedropper, remove about a teaspoon of ink and replace with essential oils. Try rose oil, lavender oil, lemon verbena, or bee balm. Attach a small card and tell them how much you love it when they write.

Housewarming Gifts

■ If you know some of the projects the new homeowners are planning to get started on right away, consider giving them a gift that helps them get started. If they have a big painting job ahead of them, how about a handful of paint brushes in varying sizes, tied with a bow? (Note: I wouldn't suggest this unless your friends have mentioned they are planning to take on a particular job. Otherwise your present may seem like a suggestion: "Wow, you guys really need to paint." This will not go over well.)

- Here's another thoughtful, and supremely affordable, housewarming gift. If you can do needlework (cross-stitch being one of the easiest varieties thereof), you can create a small piece that marks the date that your friends moved into their new home. Include their names, too. Find a simple precut, preprinted mat, with room for you to add all the appropriate information. Framing probably won't be necessary; these are usually quite lovely as is.

- Another thrifty needlepoint idea for someone moving into a new abode: A new keychain for all those new keys. Try to personalize it, either with initials or with an image of an item the recipient loves to collect.

- Here's a thoughtful housewarming gift: a big pot of stew, or anything else that will help stock the new refrigerator during that hectic first week.

- Housewarming gifts that don't cost a lot, but mean a lot, continued: Offer to take the kids to the movies while Mom and Dad paint, unpack, or otherwise orient themselves to the new surroundings. The grownups will appreciate this a lot more than that third toaster.

- Nowadays, the gift of music is pretty darn affordable. Your local department store or music outlet probably has a bargain-bin arrangement boasting some fine classic recordings (Judy Garland, Billie Holiday, Bing Crosby, Nat King Cole, etc.) in the $4–$12 range. These classic recordings can really make a home come alive. And if your friends can't dig Nat, what kind of friends are they, really?

- Is it someone's first night in a new house? How about

packing them a picnic dinner and dropping it off in person? Fill a basket or cooler with fried chicken and apple pie. Don't forget the plastic plates and tableware. You might even add a quart of milk and some cereal for the morning, too.

Wedding Showers

General strategy tip: Make this gift small and cute; save the heavy artillery for the wedding gift.

- Consider giving something for the new couple's kitchen, like a good cookie sheet and a favorite recipe for cookies. Include the first batch as part of the gift. (But use your own cookie sheet to make them!)

- Stay away from the naughty underwear. She'll get plenty, and she'll hate most of it. Instead, try bath salts meant for the day of the wedding—or the honeymoon.

- Another nice gift idea that won't break the bank: a pretty blank book with a note suggesting that the bride use the book to record all of her feelings in these special days to come. Suggest that the bride pass the book on to her daughter someday.

- Here's another supremely thoughtful, no-budget gift: a collection of your favorite recipes—and perhaps those of the other women in the wedding party. Put everything in an attractive recipe box. You've just started the new bride off with years of collective experience in cooking!

Anniversaries

- On the major anniversaries—you know, the ones that end in a five or a zero—consider making a framed, personalized piece of needlework marking the big day. If cross-stitch is your passion, put it to work!

- Are your parents or grandparents planning to celebrate their fiftieth wedding anniversary? They might get a big charge out of a personalized greeting from the President of the United States. It's free. Write (well ahead of time!) to the White House Greetings Office, Room 91, 1600 Pennsylvania Avenue, Washington, DC 20500. Even if your folks didn't vote for the current resident, it's still a kick to get mail from the White House.

- Get the other relatives in your family to donate a copy of a favorite photo of the couple. You organize an album for them from yourself and all the gang. Include captions under each picture including date, location, and any other information you'd care to add.

Baby Showers

When it comes to baby showers, I'm a firm believer in the practice of combining a number of small inexpensive gifts to make one bigger gift. This is an especially appropriate tactic when it comes to assembling gifts for babies (and their parents). New parents can be expected to have a long list of things that don't cost a lot, but that they run out of on a regular basis. Help stock them up in several areas at once. Some specific category ideas follow, but feel free to adapt the principle to some specific area not addressed below.

- Bibs, bibs, bibs. As any parent can attest, unless you've got five washing machines running at once, you can never have enough bibs. They're essential, they're cheap, and, if you're adept at sewing and cross-stitch, you can make them yourself. Combine the bib(s) you give with a first utensil kit.

- Blankets are something else newborns tend to need in quantity. One makes a very nice gift, even if someone else has the same idea. Include a small stuffed animal. You're set—and you didn't spend a bundle for the bundle!

- How about giving the contents of a baby-size medicine cabinet? This would include appropriate pain relievers, an infant thermometer, an infant nail clipper, and a teething ring. This stuff is inexpensive—and it's essential equipment for new parents. (Plus, all of it tends to get lost on a regular basis, which means duplications are no problem.)

- Another item babies tend to go through pretty quickly are those one-piece undershirts with legholes and snaps. Have your children (or the new baby's siblings) decorate the ones you give with nontoxic fabric makers. With a little guidance from you, they can create some pleasant smiling faces. Without a little guidance from you, they can go the abstract route. Your call.

- Don't forget the woman doing all the work. A small collection of soap, powder, or perfume for the mom is a welcome (and inexpensive) treat for a very pregnant mother-to-be.

- A rag doll is a classic, affordable gift for any baby, boy or girl. If you can sew, try making one out of terrycloth. This is a very easy fabric to work with, and it provides lots of tactile stimulation for the baby. Check closely for pins and other nasties before passing along the gift!

On the Baby's Arrival

- General advice: Keep it simple! (Remember, you already gave a present!)

- How about a framed newspaper from the day the child is born? Wrap with ribbon, pink or blue. Add a card.

- Short on time? Forget the expensive stuff from the hospital gift shop. Bring the new mother a milkshake when you're visiting the hospital or birth center. Trust me. She'll appreciate it.

- Along the same lines, a casserole that can be heated up later is another practical gift that costs next to nothing. These people are exhausted, and they won't be sleeping much in the near future. Cooking won't be high on the list of things they'll miss.

- Offer to babysit. Tell the new parents that you will be happy to keep an eye on the baby for their first night out on the town after the birth. Tell them to call as often as they like so that they can check in. Tell them to stay out as long as they feel comfortable. For first-time parents, this may be about half an hour. But at least you can give them a little time on their own.

- Is there a storybook you loved as a child? Consider giving a copy of the same book. Don't forget to inscribe that information in the inside front cover. Date the gift, too.

- Is there a bigger child at home who might be feeling left out? How about leading a trip to the ice cream store for that member of the family—or perhaps a package of coloring books and some new crayons?

- If you know the older child well, and he or she feels comfortable with you, you could suggest a sleep-over at your house. Rent a favorite video, and read the child a good old-fashioned story. Let him or her help you make homemade pizza.

14

Weddings

People who are planning a wedding almost never seem to take the middle road. They want either the simplest ceremony possible or something that would make Princess Di feel as though she'd skimped. Weddings are wonderful daydreams for some—and endless hassles for others.

With a little imagination and a certain sense for the timing involved, you can have a beautiful wedding, even if you're not shooting for the stars when it comes to all the trimmings. Remember Diana's wedding? Didn't it look as though she could have been having a little more fun?

- If the wedding gown is important to the bride and there isn't one being handed down from her mother or grandmother, consider the other options that are available. Many bridal shops have great clearance sales (usually only once a year). You may be able to get a $1,000 dress for $250—check for size and condition carefully, though. Look for snags, lipstick stains, and rips. As a general rule, these dresses cannot be returned if you find a flaw later on, unless you negotiate repair and alteration arrangements before you make your purchase. Bring your friends

126

to the sale to help with the inevitable trading and bartering that takes place.

■ Think twice before paying for a gown from a popular company that the store "doesn't usually carry" but "can order from with no problem." This may be a telltale sign that the store is in financial trouble and cannot keep sufficient inventory from mainstream companies on hand. Many a bride has lost a down payment by signing a check in this situation.

■ Making your gown yourself, or asking a friend or relative to? Keep it realistic. Most extravagant, dramatic effects are best left to the professionals when it comes to design (and execution, for that matter). Better to have a modest gown that does all it ought to than one that doesn't quite hit all its marks.

■ Have lots of fittings to make sure the dress is going the way you like it—*before* the important date draws too near to change it.

■ Instead of decking the entire church out with flowers (an expensive proposition), why not have the bride carry a single perfect rose? It's dazzling, it's dramatic, and it's still acceptable for throwing to the bridesmaids. Only harder to catch. Do be sure to remove those thorns.

■ Instead of expensive bouquets, give the bridesmaids fans to carry. Tie them with ribbons cascading down the front. Sandalwood scented fans can be found in your local Asian market for $5–$10 each. They can even be spray-painted to match your wedding's color.

■ If the church is to be decorated with flowers, ask the officiant if he or she would mind if you took them back for the reception.

- Have you considered buying silk flowers for the table centerpieces, or perhaps even silk ivy with a pretty candle in the center? These displays are lovely to look at, and they'll be a lot less expensive than the floral arrangements some relative you don't know will take home.

- The bride's table can use the same type of silk ivy, perhaps with some white Christmas lights (bought off-season) for accent. A surprisingly beautiful and dramatic effect for 99 cents a string!

- Some brides display perennials at the reception, then replant them after the celebration. If you're going to try this, do so at the bride's table only, where they won't be taken as party favors.

- A good friend of mine bought flowering hibiscus trees for her wedding reception and kept them for her new apartment. They look great in an apartment with little furniture (the typical newlywed dwelling).

- Need to find a way to incorporate flowers in your wedding somehow—without going to the poorhouse? You may want to consider cutting out the middleman (the florist) altogether. This will mean lots of extra work for you. But you're going to be giving yourself three to six months to plan the wedding anyway, right? This is enough time to take a class or two in flower design, or enlist a trustworthy member of the family to do it for you. Sit down together and plan what flowers you would like and where you want to use them for decorating. Then head down to the flower market and start pricing flowers. Find the best values. Ask if the flowers will be in season at the time of your wedding. Reserve what you want. Now, someone will have to go to the market the day of the wedding to pick up the flowers, *and* put everything together—that day. It's a lot to ask...but you'll save a bundle.

■ For a wedding scheduled near the Fourth of July, why not use red, white, and blue ribbon instead of expensive boutonnieres?

■ If yours is a Christmas-season wedding, how about holly as a boutonniere—and woven into wreaths for the bridesmaids' hair?

■ Florists will try to sell you every flower arrangement they can including garlands for the kitchen sink. Don't overdo the flowers. Remember, it's not the flowers the guests remember, it's the bride and groom and how welcome the guests were made to feel. One great bouquet at the front of the church or a simple red rose on each table will make as much of an impression.

■ Renting a tank of helium and a couple of dozen balloons is a fun option for decorating the reception. Ask the ushers to fill the balloons before the wedding and tell them not to inhale the helium, please. You never know what gas the tank may have held before it came into your hands. Nothing wrecks a reception like a loopy usher.

■ Try decorating your tables with simple inexpensive hurricane lamps bought at a discount shop.

Photography

■ Consider having friends take the pictures. Supply each table with disposable cameras. Then you have them developed. You'll get photos of people you know and chances are they will be more candid. You also won't have a photographer wandering around wondering who he's supposed to be shooting. These cameras now come in wedding packs.

■ Consider having a friend videotape the event. If you're not sure about their cinematic skills then ask two friends to cover both sides of the church and the reception. This can save you anywhere from $200–$1,000.

Food

■ Food for a reception at home can come in four forms: sit-down (very expensive), station service (still a cost but great for getting guests to mingle while separating vegetarian dishes from spicy to pasta from light fare), buffet (which is cheaper but often results in long waits in line), then there's the make-it-all-yourself method, or you can have the relatives help prepare the meal. This can work well for a small wedding at home, but you better be darn certain that Aunt Susan's lasagna tastes good if it's going to be the main dish, or your guests will be hungry and Aunt Susan's feelings will be hurt.

■ Keep the appetizers to a minimum. Remember that appetizers need to be served and you'll probably have to pay for the waiters.

■ If you're having the reception at a function hall, keep in mind that many of the small things are usually included: waiters, bartenders, and even deals on the cake. Shop wisely and compare costs before choosing the location.

■ Have the reception at home, either yours or someone in the family. Perhaps even a good friend will loan you the use of his or her house.

Invitations

■ Include all the info in one mailing: maps to the wedding, acceptance cards, and the invitation itself. Forget the return envelope and the tissue liners and all other unnecessary papers; keep the weight of each letter down. 32 cents vs. 55 cents may seem a small amount but it will add up. A guest list of 200 will add up to $110 as opposed to $64.

■ Try making your return notices in postcard form. At 15 cents a piece, these will only amount to $30 for a guest list of 200.

■ If you have a computer with a clip art function, try making your own invitations. They come out looking fun and less formal. With a little hand coloring here and there (using water colors or pencils) you can make an invitation that is truly personal. Take your design to one of those office print centers and have them copy it onto good quality paper you've bought yourself. Don't overlook fun papers: cloud patterns, hearts, or and even Japanese rice paper. Just make sure the surface of the paper is smooth for good quality printing.

Music

■ A DJ is always cheaper than a live band. If you pick out the music you know you're getting sounds you like. If you can get a friend to DJ for you, all the better! You may not want to grant microphone privileges, though. If you have the time to make the tapes yourself and can just put your friend in charge of turning over the tape, there will be less chance of a problem.

15

Entertaining

Once upon a time, before CD players and video rental stores, people used to *entertain one another* when they gathered socially. Apparently it was all the rage. Didn't cost much, either! Here are some examples of ways you can incorporate this strange practice yourself.

■ Why not start a regular dinner party once a month for close friends? Everyone brings a dish according to a particular ethnic theme (like Chinese or Italian). Take turns hosting the event. Make it a rule that the hosts *don't* have to cook when their turn comes around. (After all, they're setting the table and doing the dishes.) I wouldn't try this for more than three or four couples, otherwise the expenses will run fairly high. Be sure to plan carefully, or everyone may just arrive with rolls for dinner.

■ Why not gather with friends once a week or once a month for a book club, bridge club, or sewing club? It's fun, inexpensive, and there are no kids allowed.

■ Instead of going out for the evening, why not stay in with four or five close friends and rediscover the lost art of conversation?

- Consider putting on an impromptu play reading. Rediscover Shakespeare (or any other playwright you happen to have lurking about the house) and promise not to take any of it too seriously. Costumes should be made using what you can find on hand. You say the Bard doesn't fit your group? Borrow other plays (such as *Major Barbara*) from your local library.

- Try some of the games we used to play as children. How about telling a story in a round? It can be about anything. Someone starts the story. Then when that person decides to, they pass the story on to the person to their right. That second person must take the story further, but can do so in any direction that strikes his or her fancy. You might begin the game with a murder mystery, but end with a science fiction adventure.

- A variant on the above is to commit the story to a piece of paper and limit each player's contribution to a single sentence. Pass the sheet around the room; fold the paper in such a way that only the previous sentence is visible to the person writing. With larger groups, get three or four pieces of paper going at once.

- Play Murder. Everyone picks a single piece of paper out of a hat. On one piece is the word *murder*. Show no one what you've drawn. The murderer spends the evening, well, killing people. Don't worry, you'll have no messy bloodstains to clean up. The murderer simply winks at the person. That person is then dead, and prohibited from revealing the killer's identity. If you're killed, either fall to the ground dramatically, or simply take a place on the couch and announce, "I am dead." The survivors get to play detective. If you guess wrong, you're out. If you guess right, play starts again.

■ Another fun game for larger groups is Celebrity. Each person has the name of a famous person pinned or taped to his or her back. Thus, everyone knows who you are but you. You can ask anyone at the party questions about the generalities of who you might be. (No fair asking "Who am I?" until you've given the game a fair shake.) The answers should be vague as well. If someone's got "Abe Lincoln" pinned to her back, and she asks if she was in the theater, you can honestly say, "Yes, occasionally, but you didn't always enjoy it."

■ Don't forget about board games like Trivial Pursuit, Monopoly, and Scrabble—these provided hours of frugal entertainment.

■ How about a tailgate party or picnic? You don't even need an event, just a pretty view or an interesting stop on a longish trip to a shared destination. Beats stopping in at some swanky restaurant that will charge you $28.50 for three pieces of goat cheese and a sprig of imported parsley.

■ Looking for an inexpensive date that won't make you look like too much of a penny-pincher? Suggest a night volunteering at your local public television or radio station during pledge time. It's fun, it's for a good cause, and the food's usually pretty good, too.

■ Volunteer to usher for local performance arts groups—and see the show for free.

16

Pets

Pets have to be loved. Usually that's easy. Most are quite lovable, and as a result we generally refrain from eating them. Here are some ideas on how to keep that hard-earned good feeling you and Fido have built up over the years going strong... without spending a fortune in the process.

■ If you're trying to downsize your expenses and you don't already have a pet, wait to get one until you can afford the associated costs, no matter how cute the nominated pet appears to be. If you've got a child at home begging for a pet, you could try putting them off for a while and explaining the responsibilities. If all else fails, buy a goldfish.

■ Even goldfish need a safe home to live in. A filter is not necessary if you're prepared to take the little fella out, place him in another bowl of water, and change the water in his regular bowl every week or so. He will need some gravel for the bottom. And if you feel like splurging on a little ceramic castle or a plastic plant, you'll be able to keep everyone (i.e., both the goldfish and your child) happy. With proper care, your goldfish should live. For a while.

- You may be able to get away with cleaning your fish's bowl or tank less frequently if you buy a snail to keep him company. This fascinating crustacean will happily rid the sides of any algae buildup. Ask the pet shop owner for details.

- Mice, gerbils, and other small rodents are cute, furry, and not too expensive. They also have an endearing habit of escaping from their cages, never to be seen again. If you buy one of these pets, keep the top well secured at all times and change the wood chips regularly. Ask the pet shop owner for feeding details. You don't have to spend much on entertainment, either: A treadmill will keep most mice and gerbils happy for hours. They also love leftover toilet paper rolls.

- Warning: Mice and gerbils have been known to arrive at one's home already pregnant. If you're not crazy about the time and expense associated with a new rodent family, you should, before you put your money down, ask the person you buy the pet from to agree to exchange your new brood for a more chaste replacement if there turn out to be babies in the picture. Hey, it's worth a try.

- Cats are not as completely self-reliant as they would have you believe. They need affection, when they want it. A litter box, when they need it. And food, the kind they like. What kind is that? You may not know for some time. Cats need to have *access* to an indoor litter box all year round, but chances are, if they can get outside, they will use it only in cold or very wet weather. Save yourself a carpet-cleaning bill; check the litter more regularly when it starts getting chilly.

- Ask your veterinarian about the brands of cat food most likely to prevent urinary tract infections in your cats. (The bills associated with this malady can be quite impressive.) Bring some home and pour it in the bowl. Pray that they eat it.

- Thinking about buying a cute little puppy? Put in some research time at the library and find out how big that cute little puppy is likely to get—and how frisky. These are factors worth considering for apartment owners who aren't crazy about the idea of redecorating their apartment every month or two, thanks to a big, overzealous pooch they weren't expecting to have to share the place with.

- Tests have shown that bigger dogs eat more than smaller dogs. Big surprise, huh? Anyway, it's worth considering if you're trying to track down the most economical pooch.

- Do you have children? There are many pets that do not share a living place well with kids. Me, I'd avoid poodles, chows, terriers, and pit bulls. Ask your veterinarian for advice before you put any money on the table.

- Whatever you do, have your pet spayed or neutered! Don't add to your expenses by giving yourself more animal mouths to feed...unless, of course, you're prepared to assume the cost and responsibility.

- Don't buy any pet larger than a dog. It won't be cheap. Trust me.

- Immunize your pets.

- Attending to other matters of basic health care for your pet will often save you costly visits to the veterinarian later on. Ask your vet about the best preventive steps you can take to keep your pet happy and healthy.

- Make sure your pet's coat is clean and free of fleas and ticks. They'll be easier to live with, and they'll be less likely to get sick.

- Ask your vet about flea collars and chewable tablets that can help prevent fleas, ticks, and heartworm disease as well. Which is right for your pet? Investing in the right medication now can save you money later.

- Before you take your animal to the local veterinarian, check the phone book. See if there are any free animal-care clinics in your area.

- If you have more than one pet, ask your vet if there's any discount you can take advantage of by bringing them all in at the same time. If necessary, bring a friend to help you transport everyone.

- Don't bring a new pet into your house without having it checked by a vet first—even a pet you're taking care of for a day or two. You may be inviting a contagious condition into your home.

- Learn to do some grooming yourself. Washing, nail clipping, and ear cleaning are all jobs that you can probably do, rather than paying someone else. Your veterinarian may have has free advice on this score.

- Call on the phone to get advice from your vet *before* you pay for a visit.

- Following surgery or other treatment, ask your vet if your pet can recuperate at home instead of at the animal center. You'll save a great deal that way.

- Two hundred and fifty dollars to get Fido up and about again? Sure, you love Fido, but...Find out if you can spread the payments for any charges over a substantial period of time. It's just possible that this bill is not the highest on your priority list.

- Ask for details about anything you don't understand on the bill, just as you would with any hospital bill.

■ Many states and animal protection services provide assistance for getting your pet fixed and vaccinated. Ask your vet or your local animal rescue league for details.

■ Some foods that humans love (ice cream and chocolate, for instance), even in relatively small amounts, can make your pet very ill. Whenever possible, avoid tossing your pet table scraps.

■ There are many new pet food brands on the market that have been formulated to meet your pet's dietary needs more efficiently. (Science Diet and Eukanuba are two of the most popular brands in this category.) The theory is that your pet produces less waste because more of the contents of the food are used by your pet's digestion. There's little or no cereal or filler. Less of these brands of pet food may go a lot longer way for you. Even though these foods are more expensive than many grocery-store brands, this is a case where you really do get exactly what you pay for. Your pet may eat half as much of the high-quality foods, and the cost is only a few dollars more per large bag. Ask your vet for an opinion, but most will tell you that supermarket brands will not cover all your dog's or cat's dietary needs. In the long run, these new foods may prevent serious medical problems such as heart disease and will help keep your pet's coat shiny and healthy.

■ Looking for someplace that sells these new high-efficiency pet foods at a discount? Stop by one of the big pet care warehouses. Ask your veterinarian for advice on the best source.

■ If you buy your cat that Egyptian-Pharoah, deluxe, imported eel-braised-in-champagne stuff that comes in the little gold foil containers, you have only yourself to blame.

One taste and they'll be expecting it at every mealtime for the next two months.

■ Has you vet suggested a heartworm medication for your pet? If so, get a written prescription; in this case, buying through the vet is cheaper.

■ You may hear people advising you to buy prescription drugs for your pet from a veterinary medicine catalog. There are any number of potential disadvantages here. Even if you track such a catalog down (they can be quite difficult to find), they often supply products that are well past their optimum shelf life. If the medication doesn't come in a refrigerated container, it has probably already gone bad. Now, that's no deal.

17

Keeping in Touch

Sure, we love our friends and family, but do we have to pay an arm and a leg to stay in contact with them? Here are some ideas for keeping up with all the news without spending a bundle.

■ Are you looking for instant (and affordable) communication with overseas friends? Discover the wonders of e-mail. Just be careful about the premium options your on-line service provider tries to sneak in on you. Even if your friend doesn't own an Internet-friendly home computer, he or she may have access to one at work.

■ Cancel the call waiting service on your phone. Why pay to be told when a telemarketer is on the other line?

■ Calling directory assistance? The phone directory is almost certainly cheaper; there's no charge for using it more than a certain number of times per month, right? Come on. You're not in *that* much of a hurry.

■ If you do call 411, don't fall for the "we-can-connect-your-call-directly-for-a-slight-fee" trick. This can get to be an expensive habit.

- The next time you're tempted to pick up the phone and make the third long-distance phone call of the month to a close friend, why not get out a pad of paper and write a letter instead?

- One low-cost family tradition that you may want to incorporate: partial letters, a sentence or paragraph long, that the sender must extend and send back to you (or to the next person on the list). Costs less than a phone call, and there's a permanent record of the (usually lighthearted) exchange at the end of the process.

- If you do decide to phone, don't call long-distance during peak times. Call your provider for a list of the applicable rates.

- On the road? Don't get duped by those weird, no-name long-distance companies lurking within harmless looking pay phones. The rates are often hideous, even if you use your own calling card! If you don't recognize the company's name, keep going till you find a friendlier pay phone or a home phone you can use to charge your call.

- Include your Internet address (if you have one) in all your correspondence with the retailers you trust. You may get the first word of the best bargains.

- Make a personalized cassette tape and send it to a loved one. (This is a particularly nice gesture if there are small children in the house whose voices you can record for posterity.) You get an hour or so of talking time at a fraction of the cost of a phone call—and who wants to do all that listening anyway?

- Don't toss your phone-bill paperwork after you pay the bill. Hold on to the call listings for three months, then take a close look at who you are calling, how often, and at what time. Call each long-distance company and find out how its program would affect you. Then make the best call—and don't be afraid to play one company against the other. Quote the best rate you've heard about, and ask if the company you're talking to can beat it.

■ Some long-distance companies offer a substantial discount for calling at off-peak hours. Those hours may not be as "off" as they appear. If you've got relatives who live in different time zones, the supposedly "inconvenient" hours may be perfect for you.

■ Don't forget to ask the long-distance company about rebates, discounts, and other promotions. (Many promotional offers won't be extended to you unless you ask for them.)

■ If you'd like some help making sense of the sometimes confusing world of telephone costs, contact Telecommunications Research and Action Center (TRAC). It publishes a "Tele-Tips" pamphlet that will give you the lowdown on the latest rates and service options. Send $3 and a self-addressed stamped envelope to: Telecommunications Research and Action Center, P.O. Box 12038, Washington, DC 20005. The pamphlet will pay for itself after only a few calls.

18

Computers and Software

Computer stuff doesn't *have* to be expensive. Here's proof!

- Consolidate your old computer disks. Copy the files you need onto archive disks; delete the rest and format the extra disks rather than buying new blank ones.

- Shopping for a computer? Congratulations! Unless you require the most up-to-date software available—and most of us don't—you can use your local classified ads to find "used" (i.e., one-year-old) brand-name systems. Prices have been known to drop by 75 percent in a single year.

- Don't allow food or drink within about 10 feet of your computer system. One spill can pretty much fry your main processor chip and who wants to buy another one of *those*? (Besides, wouldn't you have to go to therapy or something?)

- If you're short on space and cash, consider buying software that will allow your computer to send and receive faxes, rather than buying a separate fax machine. You need a modem and printer, of course. You just plug your regular phone line into the modem. The software costs about $75—a lot less than a fax machine and a separate line to hook it up to.

Free Software on the Internet

Some of the coolest software available is known as "shareware"—which means you try the program out before you buy, and pay only if you really like it (usually in order to get a version with more features). For all of the following tips, you can go to the main Winsite page (http://winsite.com) for help on downloading and decompressing files.

- One particularly popular children's program is Amy's Fun-2-3 Adventure. You can find, and download, the program on the World Wide Web by entering the location http://www.portal.com/~devasoft into your browser and following the appropriate prompts.

- If you need help keeping up with the books—the ones on your shelf, that is—you may want to get a look at Bookworm, a Windows shareware database program especially for book collectors. Point your World Wide Web browser to http://www.winsite.com/win3/pim/ and download bk-wrm10.zip (file number 951208) and the other indicated files.

- Is keeping track of all those recipes you've been collecting for years getting a little exasperating? Download Recipe Book for Windows and give it a try. This is a shareware recipe database management program. Point your World Wide Web browser to http://www.winsite.com/win3/pim/ and download recipe2.zip (file number 950901). Go to the main Winsite page (http://winsite.com) for help on downloading and decompressing files.

- If you've got a Windows system and are interested in finding out more about your family history, try Family

Matters, a shareware genealogy program. Point your World Wide Web browser to http://www.winsite.com/ win3/pim/ and download fm2202.zip (file number 951104) and the other indicated files. Go to the main Winsite page (http://winsite.com) for help on downloading and decompressing files.

■ Need some help on the job-search front? Maybe you should incorporate Job Hunt into your campaign. It's a multifeature Windows shareware program that could just put you in front of the right employer in short order. Point your World Wide Web browser to http://www.winsite.com/win3/pim/ and download jobhn63a.zip (file number 950627) and the other indicated files. Go to the main Winsite page (http://winsite.com) for help on downloading and decompressing files.

■ Before you set out to conquer Wall Street, take a gander at BullsEye, a shareware stock-charting and portfolio management program for Windows. It may help you prioritize things—and point you toward that winning issue. Point your World Wide Web browser to http://www.winsite.com/win3/pim/ and download buleye41.zip (file number 950125). Go to the main Winsite page (http://winsite.com) for help on downloading and decompressing files.

■ What were you supposed to do? When were you supposed to do it? If you need a little help in your personal scheduling, download Full Contact. This is an advanced, customizable personal information manager. Point your World Wide Web browser to http://www.winsite.com/win3/pim/ and download fco21ea.zip (file number 950403) and the indicated companion file. Go to the main Winsite page (http://winsite.com) for help on downloading and decompressing files.

■ Watch what you're eating! And if you want to get specific about it, download the Fat, Cholesterol, and Sodium Counter. It's a shareware diet analysis program that may be right for you. Point your World Wide Web browser to http://www.winsite.com/win3/pim/ and download ngfcs41.zip (file number 951123) and the other indicated files. Go to the main Winsite page (http://winsite.com) for help on downloading and decompressing files.

■ Yeah, yeah, yeah: You're planning to score big in the office football pool. You may want to take a look at PredMan, a shareware football pool manager for Windows. Point your World Wide Web browser to http://www.winsite.com/win3/pim/ and download pmpfl2.zip (file number 950702). Go to the main Winsite page (http://winsite.com) for help on downloading and decompressing files.

■ Need some help crunching the numbers on that loan you're thinking of taking out? Take a look at LoanCalc, a shareware loan calculator for Windows. Point your World Wide Web browser to http://www.winsite.com/win3/pim/ and download loan11.exe(file number 950111). Go to the main Winsite page (http://winsite.com) for help on downloading and decompressing files.

■ Is planning your family's life getting a little too complicated for the old refrigerator-magnet-and-scrawled-note method? Take a look at Family Calendar for Windows, a shareware program that may help you simplify things around the house. Point your World Wide Web browser to http://www.winsite.com/win3/pim/ and download famcal13.zip (file number 950424). Go to the main Winsite page (http://winsite.com) for help on downloading and decompressing files.

■ If you like Scrabble, you may enjoy Mission Alphatron, a

Windows shareware game. Point your World Wide Web browser to http://www.winsite.com/win3/games/ and download alpha.zip (file number 940408). Go to the main Winsite page (http://winsite.com) for help on downloading and decompressing files.

■ Hit the slopes! You may get a kick out of Black Diamond Skiing, a shareware downhill skiing game. Point your World Wide Web browser to http://www.winsite.com/win3/games/ and download bdski11.zip (file number 950803). Go to the main Winsite page (http://winsite.com) for help on downloading and decompressing files.

■ Canasta, anyone? If you love the classic game, you may want to check out Canasta for Windows, a shareware adaptation. Point your World Wide Web browser to http://www.winsite.com/win3/games/ and download can30.exe (file number 951206). Go to the main Winsite page (http://winsite.com) for help on downloading and decompressing files.

■ If you're ready to move beyond Solitaire and Minesweeper, and you're eager for a little Vegas-style action, you may want to check out RSI Casino, a shareware game for Windows featuring blackjack and draw poker. Point your World Wide Web browser to http://www.winsite.com/win3/games/ and download casino11.zip (file number 950729). Go to the main Winsite page (http://winsite.com) for help on downloading and decompressing files.

■ Ready for a game of chess? There are a lot of good shareware programs for Windows available; you may get a kick out of Gnu Chess for Windows. Point your World Wide Web browser to http://www.winsite.com/win3/games/ and download chess321.zip (file number 910819).

Go to the main Winsite page (http://winsite.com) for help on downloading and decompressing files.

- Cribbage fans tend to go downright crazy for their game of choice; others tend to wonder what all the fuss is about. If you're a member of the former group, you may want to take a look at Cribbage for Windows, a shareware game. Point your World Wide Web browser to http://www.winsite.com/win3/games/ and download cribw11.zip (file number 950723). Go to the main Winsite page (http://winsite.com) for help on downloading and decompressing files.

- In England, the game is known as draughts; over here, we call it checkers. If you're looking for a shareware checkers game for Windows, take a look at Draughts. Point your World Wide Web browser to http://www.winsite.com/win3/games/ and download draughts.zip (file number 930216). Go to the main Winsite page (http://winsite.com) for help on downloading and decompressing files.

- It may remind you of a certain favorite childhood game. Check out S.S. Battleship, a shareware game with a twist. Point your World Wide Web browser to http://www.winsite.com/win3/games/ and download ssbatl.zip (file number 930715). Go to the main Winsite page (http://winsite.com) for help on downloading and decompressing files.

- Admit it: Like most of the rest of the world's Windows operating system users, you have yet to explore *all* of the programs that came preinstalled on your computer. If you've got a recent version of Widows, odds are you also have a graphics program (Paintbrush), a word processor (Write), a personal scheduler (Calendar), and a database manager (Cardfile). If you're considering purchasing software in any of these basic areas, and your needs aren't all that cutting-edge, you may be able to get by quite nicely with one of the programs you already have. Take a look at what you've already got before you buy something new.

■ Is there a Beatles fan on our Christmas list? Use your World Wide Web browser to soar over to http://www.primenet.com[dhaber/beatles.html/ and download some cool Fab Four software. The site includes a Windows trivia quiz, a sound player, and a screen saver.

■ The Usenet newsgroup alt.ascii,art features loads of cool graphics printable from *any* printer and *any* computer, regardless of your system! (Careful around the kids— some may be a little spicey.) Just print the item you select with a proportional font, preferably in a smaller size.

■ You say you've got a Macintosh? You, too, can get in on the shareware thing. Just use the Internet's FTP function to reach the following address: sumex-aim.stanford.edu. Once you're there, go to info-mac/*. There you'll find a bunch of great programs, including games, graphics programs, and much, much more. For a full explanation of File Transfer Protocol (the way you'll be getting into the site), see John R. Levine and Carol Baroudi's excellent book *The Internet for Dummies*.

Subscribing to Lists

Who needs to pay for magazine subscriptions? If your computer can send and receive e-mail, you can subscribe for *free* to dozens of on-line discussion groups in areas of interest to you. For instance, by sending the message SUB-SCRIBE FOOD-NET (your first name) (your last name) to majordomo@best.com you will be able to get the latest information on food safety and nutrition issues.

- By sending the message SUBSCRIBE FREE-L (your first name) (your last name) to listserv@indycms.iupui.edu you will be able to get the latest updates for divorced fathers on issues of child custody and visitation.

- By sending the message SUB ECENET-L (your first name) your last name) to listserv@vmd.cso.uiuc.edu you will be able to join a discussion group on early childhood education.

- By sending the message SUBSCRIBE SPEDTALK (your first name) (your last name) to listserv@asuvm. inre.asu.edu you will be able to join a discussion group focusing on special education issues.

- By sending the message SUB COMMUNET (your first name) (your last name) to listserv@uvmvm.uvm.edu you will be able to get the latest advice on community organizing and networking techniques.

- Looking for some help on that grant proposal? Send the message SUBSCRIBE FUNDMU-L (your first name) (your last name) to listserv@mizzoul.missouri.edu and you'll get the latest ideas from a discussion group focusing on grant and development issues.

- If you're feeling a little uncertain about your career, you may want to tap into the discussion group overseen by the National Workforce Assistance Collaborative on the changing nature of the world of employment. Just send the message SUBSCRIBE NWAC-L (your first name) (your last name) to listserv@psuvm.psu.edu and the notes will show up in your electronic mailbox.

- For a wide-ranging discussion of singles-related issues, send the message SUBSCRIBE SINGLES to majordomo@ indiana.edu and check your mailbox for the latest observations on issues such as dating, solo apartment life, and the ticking biological clock. One suspects that social engagements arise from some of the postings as well.

- If you or someone you know is dealing with issues of chronic depression, you should take a look at the Walkers in Darkness newsgroup, which can provide both support and the most recent information on dealing with depression-related problems. Just send the message SUBSCRIBE WALKERS-DIGEST to majordomo@world.std.com and keep an eye on your mailbox for the responses you receive.

- If someone you know has a family member who suffers from a disability, you may want to suggest that they send the message DIS-SPRT (first name) (last name) to listserv@sjuvm.stjohns.edu and take advantage of the support-group discussions and updates there.

- If someone you know has a disability and is interested in finding out about advocacy and Americans With Disabilities Act–related issues, tell them to send the message SUBSCRIBE ADVOCACY to listserv@sjuvm.stjohns.edu and get the latest news on this front.

- There is also a disability-related newsgroup devoted exclusively to the topic of networking. If you or someone you know is interested in subscribing, just send the message SUBSCRIBE DDFIND-L (first name) (last name) to listserv@vml.nodak.edu and monitor your mailbox for the next day or so for the electronic response.

- Want to get the latest news on diet and weight loss issues? Just send the message FIT-L (your first name) (your last name) to listserv@etsuadmn.etsu.edu and keep an eye on your mailbox for the electronic response you receive.

- If you have questions about learning disabilities, there is an on-line discussion group you should consider joining. Just send a message to LD-List-Request%mvac23@louie. udel.edu asking to join the learning disabilities list.

■ To get the latest information on longevity and aging issues, send the message SUB LONGEVITY (your first name) (your last name) to listserv@vm3090.ege.edu.tr and monitor your electronic mailbox for the response.

■ Do you have questions about the prescription drug Prozac? You're not alone. To subscribe to an on-line discussion group dealing with this issue, send the message SUB PROZAC (your first name) (your last name) to listserv@s-juvm.stjohns.edu and monitor your electronic mailbox for the response.

■ If you are a prospective or current parent with questions about the legal issues surrounding adoption, you should subscribe to the on-line newsgroup dealing with this topic. To do so, just send the message SUBSCRIBE ADOPTION (your first name) (your last name) to listserv@listserv.law.cornell.edu and keep an eye on your electronic mailbox for the reply you receive.

■ If you are an adoptee who'd like to find out more about your rights, send the message SUBSCRIBE ADOPTEES (your first name) (your last name) to adoptees-request@ucsd and you'll receive the latest on-line discussions on this topic.

■ If you're a member of Amnesty International and would like to join that group's on-line discussion list, send the message SUBSCRIBE AIMEMBERS-L (your e-mail address) to majordomo@lists.best.com and keep an eye on your electronic mailbox for the response you receive.

19

Your Rights

Push *you* around? I'd like to see 'em try. In this chapter, you'll find a brief review of some of the most important ways you can save yourself money (and aggravation) by exercising your rights as a consumer.

Warranties and Guarantees

Don't sign the check yet! Read the warranty or guarantee closely. The following advice on warranties and guarantees, courtesy of the U.S. Office of Consumer Affairs, is worth reviewing closely before any major purchase.

- Don't wait until the product fails or needs repair to find out what the warranty covers.

- Does the product cost $15 or more? If so, the law says that the seller *must* let you examine any warranty before you make a purchase. But you have to ask. Review all relevant terms and conditions of warranties or guarantees *before* you put your money down.

- Ask how long the warranty lasts, and when it begins.

- What parts and what particular problems are covered?

- Will the warranty pay for 100 percent of repair costs—or simply parts, with you footing the bill for labor?

- Will the warranty pay for testing the product before it is repaired?

- Will the warranty pay for shipping?

- Will the warranty pay for a replacement model for you to use while the product is being repaired?

- Is any action required on your part to activate the warranty, and what time frame must you act within?

- Are regular inspections or maintenance required to activate the warranty?

- Will you personally have to ship the product somewhere in order to get it repaired?

- Is the manufacturer or the retailer offering the warranty?

- How long has the entity offering the warranty been in business? This may be an indication of reliability.

Dealing With Debt

- If you're behind on your mortgage payments and worried about losing your house, call the U.S. Department of Housing and Urban Development right away and order a copy of *Saving Your Home*, a publication that will show you how to avoid losing your dwelling. Call the Department at 202-401-0388, or call the U.S. Government Printing Office at 202-512-1800.

- Remember: It's not the end of the world to owe someone money! They can't put you on the rack, or take your kids away, or drop a bomb on you. So rule one is, *don't dodge the calls*. When you're contacted by creditors or their representatives, make it clear that you *want to pay the money back and are doing your best to work out repayment plans that will satisfy the creditor.* Make sure that message gets through. Legal action is far less likely to take place if you make this clear to creditors. As a general rule, creditors save the attorney's fees for the people who owe the most money *and* ignore all reasonable attempts to work out payment arrangements.

■ Legally, collection agencies may not call you before 8:30 in the morning. If they do, it's harassment. Tell the callers this in no uncertain terms. Don't get flustered. Keep your cool. Remind the person of the rules. Disengage. Mark the details of the call, including the time and the name of the caller, in a notebook. If a pattern of early calling emerges, call a lawyer. You may have a nice fat lawsuit on your hands.

■ If an agent is out-and-out rude to you on the phone, or threatens you in any way, give yourself a pat on the back. You are now in control of the situation. The law and the courts are on your side: Harassing collection calls are a no-no, and most agencies know it. *Immediately* ask for the name of the person who was abusive to you. Be sure to get any appropriate identification numbers or direct phone numbers. Then ask to speak to the supervisor. If the person refuses, hang up. Call the agency back and demand to speak with a supervisor. Calmly tell the supervisor how rude the agent was, and inform him or her that you don't want to call the state attorney general's office about harassment, but that you will if you have no other option. Identify the offender by name. Keep you cool. Call the state attorney general's office if you must.

■ If the collector falsely claims to represent a government agency, contact your state attorney general's office immediately. This technique is illegal; if a collector uses it against you, you may be in an extremely powerful position legally.

- If the collector suggests that jail time awaits you because you have failed to pay a debt, contact your state attorney general's office immediately. This, too, may put you in the driver's seat legally.

- If the collector attacks your reputation with others by publicizing your debt, or even sends overdue notices on postcards rather than in envelopes, he or she may be in serious legal trouble. Punitive measures that publicize your status as a debtor are a no-no. Contact your state attorney general's office for details.

- Here's the biggie! The collector *must* accede to your request to keep your account information private. If you spot even a minor violation of this part of the law, contact your state attorney general's office immediately.

- When push comes to shove, the creditor has only three options, two of which costs lots of money. The creditor can take you to court, which can be unbelievably expensive, especially if you have a good attorney. The creditor can also refer your account to a collection agency, but this means writing off a good chunk of the debt. Or the creditor can set up a payment plan with you. The third option is the best for everyone, no matter how much bluster or how many vague threats you hear. If you get out in front of the issue and make it clear that you *want* to pay the debt back and have ideas as to how to do so, you can usually avoid the first two options.

- If you've been denied a loan because of a bad credit report, you have a legal right to see what's on the report. Ask the lender to identify the credit bureaus that supplied the information. Contact the bureau and ask to see a copy of your report. Under the Fair Credit Reporting Act, you may challenge any inaccurate items; as long as your challenges are not "frivolous," *the bureau must remove any items it cannot verify.* So if a debt you have paid down to $250 is still listed at its original level of $1,250, you can (and should!) challenge the report.

Complaint Letters

■ Writing a complaint letter? Keep it to one page, and keep a copy for your records. Multipage rants often get filed (or tossed) rather than read.

■ When writing to seek action on a faulty product or on lousy service you've received, there is a certain strategic advantage to making a threat, veiled or otherwise, of legal action. Even if you don't plan to follow through on your lawsuit, a piece of paper that lands on someone's desk with the words "my attorney" *has to be dealt with somehow.* It's really quite remarkable how this simple technique can wake up a drowsy bureaucracy.

■ Whenever possible, specify dates, prices, and people you dealt with. If you can, enclose photocopies of receipts or canceled checks with your one-page letter.

■ State the name of the product or service you are having trouble with in the very first line, and *briefly* outline the problem you face now. This information should constitute the opening paragraph of your letter, and it should be no more than one or two short sentences long. Be sure this part of the letter stands out from the rest of the text on your single-page complaint letter.

■ Near the end of your single-page letter, state, in a single sentence, exactly what you want the organization to do next.

- List your complete contact information at the very bottom of your one-page letter, including your address and daytime and evening telephone numbers. Don't assume that a return address on your envelope will be enough.

- Always date your letter.

- Take the time to call the organization directly and ask for the name and address of the president of the company. Send this person a copy of your letter—or, if you're feeling really frustrated, address it to the president directly!

- If nothing happens, keep up the pressure. Keep writing one-page letters. Keep copies of every letter you send. Leaving a paper trail is important if you plan legal action somewhere down the line. Cite the dates of all the letters you have written in the past. It's okay to call, too, but a chain of insistent letters, followed up with brief, concise calls, is your best bet from a legal standpoint. (And they're cheaper than spending a half hour on hold, too.)

- If, after a half dozen or so letters or follow-up calls, you still have not received satisfaction, it's time to put your tax dollars to work. Write a (polite!) letter to the state attorney general's office explaining your problem. This letter, too, should be no more than one page long—but it should be accompanied by photocopies of all of the letters you've sent to the company that's trying to give you the shaft. (Send copies of your own copies. Always keep at least one photocopy of everything you send out!) Follow up appropriately by phone a few days later.

Other Consumer Rights Issues

- Having problems prying money out of your insurance company—money that's rightfully yours? It's a common (and frustrating) experience. Call the National Insurance

Consumer Hotline at 800-942-4242 and give them the details of your complaint. They'll point you in the right direction.

■ Think twice—and then three times, and then four— before signing on with any "employment consultant" who charges you, rather than the employer, for supposedly hooking you up to some "database" of interviews. Many of these operations are shady undertakings designed to charge you an arm and a leg to "develop resumés" and "initiate mailings" on your behalf. Typically, no job results. Most (not all, but most) reputable employment services, such as executive search firms, charge the employer, rather than the applicant, for their services.

■ Looking for a job? Before you consider relocating, you may want to call the government's Career America Hotline. It outlines federal employment opportunities in your area. You're a taxpayer, so you paid for this! The number: 912-757-3000.

■ Are you a veteran, or a dependent of a veteran? If so, you may be entitled to benefits you're not currently receiving. Call the U.S. Government Printing Office and order a copy of *Federal Benefits for Veterans and Dependents*. It's only $3.25, and it may just point you toward thousands of dollars in federal funds to which you are lawfully entitled.

■ Are you considering investing in a franchise opportunity? If so, you'll need to be sure you're not dealing with a shady franchise operation, of which there are many. The $21 you'll spend on the *Franchise Opportunities Handbook*, available from the U.S. Government Printing Office (or through your local library for free), will help you avoid potentially catastrophic mistakes with your investment. Call 202-512-1800 to order.

- Find out about your rights as a credit consumer. Read *The Consumer Handbook to Credit Protection Laws*. Write the Federal Reserve System Board of Governors at MS-138, Washington, DC 20551, and ask for your free copy.

- If you've bought a boat and are having trouble with a safety-related defect that the manufacturer is unable or unwilling to resolve, call the U.S. Coast Guard's Boating Safety Hotline at 800-368-5647 and report the problem. You may speed things up a bit.

- If you believe that you've been denied a job you deserve because of an employer's unwillingness to make reasonable accommodations to your disability, you should contact the Equal Employment Opportunity Commission to learn about your options. The address is 1801 L Street NW, Washington, DC 20507. Or call 800-800-3302 (TDD).

- If you have a disability and need to adapt your home to your needs, you may be eligible for a Title I Home Improvement Loan insured by the U.S. Department of Housing and Urban Development. For more information, write to: Assisted, Elderly, and Handicapped Program, Department of Housing and Urban Development, 451 7th Street SW, Room 6116, Washington, DC 20410.

- If you have served in the military and are considering purchasing a home, contact the Department of Veterans Affairs about securing a VA-guaranteed home loan. The number is 800-827-1000.

- People with disabilities who are interested in going into business for themselves may qualify for federal assistance and low-cost loans from the Small Business Administration. Call the SBA office in your area, or write to: Small Business Administration, Financial Assistance Division,

Handicapped Assistance Loan Program, Suite 8300, 409 3rd Street SW, Washington, DC 20416.

■ You say the powers that be are intent upon foisting some toxic treatment plant into a residential area? You say your property values are about to plummet? Call 800-542-1918 and ask for a copy of *The Environmentalist's Guide to the Public Library,* an indispensable (and free!) guide to local resources that will put the information you need at your fingertips.

■ Ordering something by mail? Don't get fooled into paying extra for "insuring" the delivery. If the package is damaged or lost in transit, the shipper must bear the resulting costs, not you.

■ No matter how busy things get, you have a right to do something nice for yourself at least once a day, Hey, life is short.

Bibliography

Bernstein, Peter, and Christopher Ma. *The Practical Guide to Practically Everything* (New York: Random House, 1995).

Boetig, Donna E. "Don't Pay for It—Trade for It!" *Money*, Apr. 4, 1995, p. 47.

Bryant Quinn, Jane. "Savings Bonds." *Woman's Day*, Nov. 1, 1995, p. 36.

Carter, Mary Randolph, "American Junk." *American Home Style*, Jan./Feb. 1994, p. 61.

Chelser, Bernice. *In and Out of Boston With (or Without) Children.* (Chester, Conn.: Globe Pequot Press, 1982).

Child, Maria. *The American Housewife* (Boston: Carter, Hende and Co., 1833).

Consumer Law Foundation. *The Complete Small Business Loan Kit* (Holbrook, Mass.: Bob Adams Publishers, 1990).

Cusick, Dawn. *Nature Crafts With a Microwave* (New York: Sterling Publishing Co., 1994).

Dyer, Ceil. *Best Recipes.* (New York: Galahad Books, 1989).

The editors and experts of *Bottom Line Personal. The Book of Inside Information* (New York: Boardroom Classics, 1991).

Emling, Shelley. "Last Minute Mailing Strategies." *Good Housekeeping*, Dec. 1995, p. 226.

Gallagher, Nora. *Simple Pleasures* (Reading, Mass.: Addison-Wesley Publishing Co., 1981).

Gowen, Anne. "Forty Best Ideas From America's Penny-pinchers." *Money*, Apr. 4, 1995, p. 51.

"A Guide to Auto Insurance." *Consumer Reports*, Oct. 1995, p. 638.

Hamburg, Joan. "How to Get It Wholesale." *Family Circle*, Aug. 8, 1995, p. 68.

Herbers, Jill. "Painted Walls and Floors." *Weekend Decorator*, Winter 1994, p. 55.

———. "Window Treatments." *Weekend Decorator*, Winter 1994, p. 59.

Herringbone, Barry, and Beth Christens. *Unbelievably Good Deals That You Absolutely Can't Get Unless You're a Teacher.* (Chicago: Contemporary Books, 1995).

"The Home Office: You Do It!" *Family Circle*, Fall 1995, p. 67.

Kandaswami, Chithan "Vitamin Visionaries." *Longevity*, Nov. 1995, p. 86.

Lesko, Matthew, with Mary Ann Martello, *Free Goodies and Cheapies* (Kensington, Md., Information USA, Inc., 1994.)

Levine, Elyse R. D. "Healthy Goods on a Budget." *Health Journal*, Winter 1996, p. 14.

Levine, John R., and Carol Baroudi. *The Internet for Dummies* (San Mateo, Calif.: IDG Books Worldwide, 1993).

Luloff, Howard. "Make Your Own Breakfast Cereal." *Mother Earth News*, Nov. 1995, p. 11.

Marquardt, Deborah. "Fourteen Ways to Stretch Your Paycheck." *Family Circle*, Aug. 8, 1995, p. 65.

Marques, Rose. "School of Hard Knocks." *Stages*, Fall 1995, p. 2.

Massachusetts Electric and Gas Utilities, *Maintaining an Energy Efficient Home* (Massachusetts Electric and Gas Utilities).

National Heart, Lung and Blood Institute. *Step by Step* (National Institutes of Health, Aug. 1994).

National Institutes of Health. *Eating for Life* (US Department of Health and Human Services, June 1988).

Office of Public Affairs. "Publications of National Park Services," in *The National Parks Index* (Washington, D.C.: U.S. Government Printing Office, 1993).

Paine, Melanie. *Fabric Magic* (New York: Pantheon Books, 1987).

Peel, Kathy. "Mom, I'm Bored!" *Family Circle*, June 27, 1995, p. 79.

Philcox, Phil. *Secrets of a Supershopper.* (Boca Raton, Fla.: Globe Communications, 1994).

Quint, Gilder, Barbara. "Eight Ways to Invest $1,000." *Family Circle*, June 27, 1995, p. 43.

Ramsey, Marshall. "How to Cut an Easy Ten Pounds the Natural Way," Dec. 1995, p. 12.

Reader's Digest. *Illustrated Guide to Gardening* (Pleasantville, NY: Reader's Digest Association, 1991).

Rini, Niki. "A Red Carpet for a Green Thumb." *Mother Earth News,* Nov. 1995, p. 10.

Rock, Andrea. "Hitting the Books." *Stages,* Fall 1995, p. 4.

Rowland, Mary. "Zap Credit Card Debt." *Woman's Day,* Sept. 19, 1995, p. 30.

Samtur, Susan. "Cut Your Grocery Bill in Half." *Family Circle,* Sept. 19, 1995, p. 36.

Stein, Janet. "Boo! Halloween '95." *Child,* Oct. 1995, p. 133.

Steinback, Robert. *Out of Debt* (Holbrook, Mass.: Bob Adams Publishers, 1989).

Toropov, Brandon, and Michelle Bevilacqua. *The Everything Christmas Book* (Holbrook, Mass.: Bob Adams Publishers, 1994).

Tyson, Eric. *Personal Finance for Dummies* (San Mateo, Calif.: IDG Books Worldwide, 1994).

U.S. Department of Agriculture. *Eating Better When Eating Out,* (Washington, D.C.: U.S. Government Printing Office,).

U.S. Department of Agriculture. *How Does Living Alone Affect Dietary Quality,* Oct., 1994. Washington, D.C. 20250.

U.S. Department of Agriculture, Human Nutrition Information Services. *Shopping for Food and Making Meals in Minutes,* a Home and Garden Bulletin (Washington, D.C.: U.S. Government Printing Office,).

U.S. Department of Education. *Pocket Guide to Federal Help for Individuals With Disabilities* (Washington, D.C.: U.S. Government Printing Office, 1993).

U.S. Department of Education. "Preparing Your Child For College," in *Consumer Information Catalogue* (Pueblo, Colo.: U.S. Department of Education, 1995).

U.S. Department of Housing and Urban Development. *Home Buyer's Vocabulary* (Washington, D.C.: U.S. Government Printing Office, March 1987).

U.S. Department of Labor, Bureau of Labor Statistics. "Is There Another Degree in Your Future?" *Occupational Outlook Quarterly,* Winter 1993–94.

U.S. Government. "Publications, Periodicals, Electronic Products," *U.S. Government Information Catalog*, vol. 12, no. 1, Sum-
mer/Fall 1995.

Vincent, Patrick. *Free Stuff From the Internet* (Scottsdale, Ariz.:
Coriolis Group Books, 1994).

Vivian, John. "Pellet Stoves: Wood Energy for All." *Mother Earth
News*, Nov. 1995, p. 30.

———. "Update for 1995 Wood Heat." *Mother Earth News*, Nov.
1995, p. 38.

Westland, Pamela. *Celebrating Christmas* (Vancouver, British Columbia: Annes Publishing, 1994).

More Cheapskate's Books
From Carol Publishing Group

Ask for the titles listed below at your local bookstore. Or to order direct from the publisher call 1-800-447-BOOK (MasterCard or Visa) or send a check or money order for the book purchased (plus $4.00 shipping and handling for the first book ordered and 75¢ for each additional book) to Carol Publishing Group, 120 Enterprise Avenue, Dept. 1795, Secaucus, NJ 07094

The Cheapskate's Guide to Las Vegas
Connie Emerson

Sound advice on how to get maximum satisfaction with minimum expenditure when visiting the "city without clocks." Readers will find a wealth of tips from getting a good airline fare to getting around the city to visiting nearby places of interest. Complete with money saving information on Moderately priced restaurants • The best values for shopping in hotels and malls • Tips on top attractions and entertainment–how to find the best deals, as well as how to enjoy lounge shows without paying a cent • The best places to gamble • And much, much more.
$9.95 paper (#51530)

The Cheapskate's Guide to London
Connie Emerson

Tips on the best discount shopping, attractive low-priced restaurants, deals for theater tickets and bargains on hotel and bed-and-board accommodations. The book also offers detailed information on the city's parks and museums. There are tips on wonderful day trips to Oxford, Tunbridge Wells, Alfriston, and the delights of Brighton, one of the world's premier resort areas. There is advice and tricks for maneuvering through the London transit system–one of the world's most efficient ...and best priced. This book will give you all the information you need to have a four star vacation at a one star price.
$9.95 paper (#51655)

The Cheapskate's Guide to Living Cheaper and Better
Leslie Hamilton

With this book, readers can reduce cash flow without lowering their standard of living. Chapter headings include • Home–Decorate, clean and repair to improve value • Car–What to repair, and what not to, to maintain its value • Presents–Wrapping them on the cheap, making homemade gifts look better than store-bought • All in the timing–When to burn wood for heat, when to sell stuff to get the best price • Vacations–Seasonal ideas that will make a trip cheaper and more enjoyable • And more.
$9.95 paper (#51795)

The Cheapskate's Guide to Paris
Connie Emerson

The term Paris bargain need not be an oxymoron. Though the City of Light has the (deserved) reputation of being one of the most expensive vacation locations in the world, it can also be a cost cutter's delight, provided a traveler does his homework. Readers will learn how to get maximum value for their francs, on everything from shopping to sightseeing to entertainment. This book includes tips on how to take advantage of senior citizen discounts as well as places to entertain children. It offers a key to the parks and museums that make Paris the jewel city of the world and reveals which attractions offer free admission.
$9.95 paper (#51736)

Prices subject to change; books subject to availability